WILLIAM BLAKE (1757–1827) was an English painter, poet and printmaker. He is considered a seminal figure in the history of the poetry and visual arts of the Romantic Age. In 2002, Blake was placed at number 38 in the BBC's poll of the 100 Greatest Britons. Except for a period of three years spent in Felpham, Blake lived in London for his entire life. Nevertheless, he produced a diverse and symbolically rich oeuvre, which embraced the imagination as "the body of God" or "human existence itself".

Although criticised by some contemporaries for his idiosyncratic views, Blake is held in high esteem by later critics for his expressiveness and creativity, and for the philosophical and mystical undercurrents within his work. His poetry has been characterised as part of the Romantic movement and as "Pre-Romantic". Influenced by the ideals and ambitions of the French and American revolutions, he turned against the Church of England but respected the Bible. He was influenced by thinkers like Emanuel Swendenborg. Blake had a complex relationship with Enlightenment philosophy. Owing to his visionary religious beliefs, he opposed the Newtonian view of the universe. This mindset is reflected in Blake's poem "Jerusalem". Because of the diversity of his views, critics found it difficult to classify him as a thinker.

Blake also experimented with relief etching, a method he used to produce most of his books, paintings, pamphlets and poems. The process is also referred to as illuminated printing, and the finished products as illuminated books or prints, which involved writing the text of the poems on copper plates with pens and brushes, using an acid-resistant medium.

The 19th-century scholar, William Rossetti called him a "glorious luminary", and "a man not forestalled by predecessors, nor to be classed with contemporaries, nor to be replaced by known or readily surmisable successors". Lucas said of him: "Shall I call him artist or genius–or mystic–or madman?" Samuel Taylor Coleridge considered Blake "a man of genius", and Wordsworth made his own copies of several of Blake's songs. As a Romantic writer he has exerted the most powerful influence on the 20th and the 21st centuries.

William Blake
SELECTED POEMS

William Blake

ATLANTIC
PUBLISHERS & DISTRIBUTORS (P) LTD

Published by
ATLANTIC
PUBLISHERS & DISTRIBUTORS (P) LTD
7/22, Ansari Road, Darya Ganj, New Delhi-110002
Phones : +91-11-40775252, 23273880, 23275880, 23280451
Fax : +91-11-23285873
Web : www.atlanticbooks.com
E-mail : orders@atlanticbooks.com

Branch Office
5, Nallathambi Street, Wallajah Road, Chennai-600002
Phones : +91-44-64611085, 32413319
E-mail : chennai@atlanticbooks.com

First Published 1827

Printed in India at Nice Printing Press, A-33/3A, Site-IV,
Industrial Area, Sahibabad, Ghaziabad, U.P.

CONTENTS

POETICAL SKETCHES

To Spring

O thou with dewy locks, who lookest down
Thro' the clear windows of the morning, turn
Thine angel eyes upon our western isle,
Which in full choir hails thy approach, O Spring!

The hills tell each other, and the list'ning
Vallies hear; all our longing eyes are turned
Up to thy bright pavilions: issue forth,
And let thy holy feet visit our clime.

Come o'er the eastern hills, and let our winds
Kiss thy perfumed garments; let us taste
Thy morn and evening breath; scatter thy pearls
Upon our love-sick land that mourns for thee.

O deck her forth with thy fair fingers; pour
Thy soft kisses on her bosom; and put
Thy golden crown upon her languish'd head,
Whose modest tresses were bound up for thee!

To Winter

'O Winter! bar thine adamantine doors:
The north is thine; there hast thou built thy dark
Deep-founded habitation. Shake not thy roofs.
Nor bend thy pillars with thine iron car.'

He hears me not, but o'er the yawning deep
Rides heavy; his storms are unchain'd, sheathed
In ribbed steel; I dare not lift mine eyes,
For he hath rear'd his sceptre o'er the world.

Lo! now the direful monster, whose skin clings
To his strong bones, strides o'er the groaning rocks:
He withers all in silence, and his hand
Unclothes the earth, and freezes up frail life.

He takes his seat upon the cliffs; the mariner
Cries in vain. Poor little wretch! that deal'st
With storms! till heaven smiles, and the monster
Is driv'n yelling to his caves beneath mount Hecla.

To the Evening Star

Thou fair-hair'd angel of the evening,
Now, while the sun rests on the mountains, light
Thy bright torch of love; thy radiant crown
Put on, and smile upon our evening bed!
Smile on our loves, and while thou drawest the
Blue curtains of the sky, scatter thy silver dew
On every flower that shuts its sweet eyes
In timely sleep. Let thy west wind sleep on
The lake; speak silence with thy glimmering eyes,
And wash the dusk with silver. Soon, full soon,
Dost thou withdraw; then the wolf rages wide,
And the lion glares through the dun forest:
The fleeces of our flocks are cover'd with
Thy sacred dew: protect with them with thine influence.

Song

How sweet I roam'd from field to field,
    And tasted all the summer's pride
Till the prince of love beheld
    Who in the sunny beams did glide!

He shew'd me lilies for my hair,
    And blushing roses for my brow;
He led me through his gardens fair,
    Where all his golden pleasures grow.

With sweet May dews my wings were wet,
    And Phœbus fir'd my vocal rage;
He caught me in his silken net,
    And shut me in his golden cage.

He loves to sit and hear me sing,
    Then, laughing, sports and plays with me;

Then stretches out my golden wing,
And mocks my loss of liberty.

Song

My silks and fine array,
My smiles and languish'd air,
By love are driv'n away;
And mournful lean Despair
Brings me yew to deck my grave:
Such end true lovers have.

His face is fair as heav'n
When springing buds unfold;
O why to him was 't giv'n,
Whose heart is wintry cold?
His breast is love's all-worship'd tomb,
Where all love's pilgrims come.

Bring me an axe and spade,
Bring me a winding sheet;
When I my grave have made
Let winds and tempests beat:
Then down I'll, lie, as cold as clay.
True love doth pass away!

Song

Love and harmony combine,
And around our souls! intwine,
While thy branches mix with mine,
And our roots together join.

Joys upon our branches sit,
Chirping loud and singing sweet;
Like gentle streams beneath our feet
Innocence and virtue meet.

Thou the golden fruit dost bear,
I am clad in flowers fair;
Thy sweet boughs perfume the air,
And the turtle buildeth there.

There she sits and feeds her young,
Sweet I hear her mournful song;
And thy lovely leaves among,
There is love: I hear his tongue.

There his charming nest doth lay,
There he sleeps the night away;
There he sports along the day,
And doth among our branches play.

Song

I love the jocund dance,
 The softly-breathing song,
Where innocent eyes do glance,
 And where lisps the maiden's tongue.

I love the laughing vale,
 I love the echoing hill,
Where mirth does never fail,
 And the jolly swain laughs his fill.

I love the pleasant cot,
 I love the innocent bow'r,
Where white and brown is our lot,
 Or fruit in the mid-day hour.

I love the oaken seat,
 Beneath the oaken tree,
Where all the old villagers meet,
 And laugh our sports to see.

I love our neighbours all,
 But, Kitty, I better love thee;
And love them I ever shall;
 But thou art all to me.

Song

Memory, hither come,
 And tune your merry notes;
And, while upon the wind
 Your music floats,

I'll pore upon the stream
Where sighing lovers dream,
And fish for fancies as they pass
Within the watery glass.

I'll drink of the clear stream,
And hear the linnet's song;
And there I'll lie and dream
The day along:
And when night comes, I'll go
To places fit for woe,
Walking along the darken'd valley
With silent Melancholy.

Mad Song

The wild winds weep,
And the night is a-cold;
Come hither, Sleep,
And my griefs infold:
But lo! the morning peeps
Over the eastern steeps,
And the rustling birds of dawn
The earth do scorn.

Lo! to the vault
Of paved heaven,
With sorrow fraught
My notes are driven:
They strike the ear of night,
Make weep the eyes of day;
They make mad the roaring winds,
And with tempests play.

Like a fiend in a cloud,
With howling woe,
After night I do croud,
And with night will go;
I turn my back to the east
From whence comforts have increas'd;
For light doth seize my brain
With frantic pain.

To the Muses

Whether on Ida's shady brow,
Or in the chambers of the East,
The chambers of the sun, that now
From ancient melody have ceas'd;

Whether in Heav'n ye wander fair,
Or the green corners of the earth,
Or the blue regions of the air
Where the melodious winds have birth;

Whether on crystal rocks ye rove,
Beneath the bosom of the sea
Wand'ring in many a coral grove,
Fair Nine, forsaking Poetry!

How have you left the ancient love
That bards of old enjoy'd in you!
The languid strings do scarcely move!
The sound is forc'd, the notes are few!

ALL RELIGIONS ARE ONE

The Voice of One Crying in the Wilderness

The Argument. As the true method of knowledge is experiment, the true faculty of knowing must be the faculty which experiences. This faculty I treat of.

Principle I. That the Poetic Genius is the true Man, and that the body or outward form of Man is derived from the Poetic Genius. Likewise that the forms of all things are derived from their Genius, which by the Ancients was call'd an Angel & Spirit & Demon.

Principle II. As all men are alike in outward form, So (and with the same infinite variety) all are alike in the Poetic Genius.

Principle III. No man can think, write or speak from his heart, but he must intend truth. Thus all sects of Philosophy are from the Poetic Genius adapted to the weaknesses of every individual.

Principle IV. As none by travelling over known lands can find out the unknown, So from already acquired knowledge Man could not acquire more; therefore an universal Poetic Genius exists.

Principle V. The Religions of all Nations are derived from each Nation's different reception of the Poetic Genius, which is every where call'd the Spirit of Prophecy.

Principle VI. The Jewish & Christian Testaments are An original derivation from the Poetic Genius. This is necessary from the confined nature of bodily sensation.

Principle VII. As all men are alike (tho' infinitely various), So all Religions , &, as all similars, have one source. The true Man is the source, he being the Poetic Genius.

THERE IS NO NATURAL RELIGION

(a)

The Argument. Man has no notion of moral fitness but from Education. Naturally he is only a natural organ subject to Sense.

I. Man cannot naturally Percieve but through his natural or bodily organs.

II. Man by his reasoning power can only compare & judge of what he has already perciev'd.

III. From a perception of only 3 senses or 3 elements none could deduce a fourth or fifth.

IV. None could have other than natural or organic thoughts if he had none but organic perceptions.

V. Man's desires are limited by his perceptions; none can desire what he has not perceiv'd.

VI. The desires & perceptions of man, untaught by anything but organs of sense, must be limited to objects of sense.

(b)

I. Man's perceptions are not bounded by organs of perception; he perceives more than sense (tho' ever so acute) can discover.

II. Reason, or the ratio of all we have already known, is not the same that it shall be when we know more.

III. [*This proposition is missing.*]

IV. The bounded is loathed by its possessor. The same dull round, even of a universe, would soon become a mill with complicated wheels.

V. If the many become the same as the few when possess'd, More! More! is the cry of a mistaken soul; less than All cannot satisfy Man.

VI. If any could desire what he is incapable of possessing, despair must be his eternal lot.

VII. The desire of Man being Infinite, the possession is Infinite & himself Infinite.

Conclusion. If it were not for the Poetic or Prophetic character the Philosophic & Experimental would soon be at the ratio of all things, & stand still unable to do other than repeat the same dull round over again.

Application. He who sees the Infinite in all things sees God. He who sees the Ratio only sees himself only.

Therefore God becomes as we are, that we may be as he is.

ANNOTATIONS TO LAVATER

Mark that I do not believe there is such a thing litterally, but hell is the being shut up in the possession of corporeal desires which shortly weary the man, for ALL LIFE IS HOLY.

*

It is the God in *all* that is our companion & friend, for our God himself says: 'you are my brother, my sister & my mother', & St John: 'Whoso dwelleth in love dwelleth in God & God in him' & such an one cannot judge of any but in love... God is in the lowest effects as well as in the highest causes; for he is become a worm that he may nourish the weak. For let it be remember'd that creation is God descending according to the weakness of man, for our Lord is the word of God & everything on earth is the word of God & in its essence is God.

SONGS OF INNOCENCE AND OF EXPERIENCE

Shewing the Two Contrary States of the Human Soul

SONGS OF INNOCENCE

Introduction

Piping down the valleys wild,
Piping songs of pleasant glee,
On a cloud I saw a child,
And he laughing said to me:

'Pipe a song about a Lamb.'
So I piped with merry chear.
'Piper, pipe that song again.'
So I piped, he wept to hear.

' Drop thy pipe, thy happy pipe
Sing thy songs of happy chear.'
So I sung the same again,
While he wept with joy to hear.

'Piper, sit thee down and write
In a book that all may read.'
So he vanish'd from my sight.
And I pluck'd a hollow reed.

And I made a rural pen,
And I stain'd the water clear,
And I wrote my happy songs
Every child may joy to hear.

The Shepherd

How sweet is the Shepherd's sweet lot!
From the morn to the evening he strays;
He shall follow his sheep all the day,
And his tongue shall be filled with praise.

For he hears the lamb's innocent call,
And he hears the ewe's tender reply;

He is watchful while they are in peace,
For they know when their Shepherd is nigh.

The Ecchoing Green

The Sun does arise,
And make happy the skies;
The merry bells ring
To welcome the Spring;
The sky-lark and thrush,
The birds of the bush,
Sing louder around
To the bells' chearful sound,
While our sports shall be seen
On the Ecchoing Green.

Old John, with white hair
Does laugh away care,
Sitting under the oak
Among the old folk.
They laugh at our play,
And soon they all say:
"Such, such were the joys
When we all, girls & boys,
In our youth time were seen
On the Ecchoing Green."

Till the little ones, weary,
No more can be merry;
The sun does descend,
And our sports have on end.
Round the laps of their mothers
Many sisters and brothers,
Like birds in their nest,
Are ready for rest;
And sport no more seen
On the darkening Green.

The Lamb

Little Lamb,who made thee?
Dost thou know who made thee?
Gave thee life, & bid thee feed
By the stream & o'er the mead;
Gave thee clothing of delight,
Softest clothing, wooly, bright;
Gave thee such a tender voice,
Making all the vales rejoice?
Little Lamb, who made thee?
Dost thou know who made thee?
Little Lamb, I'll tell thee,
Little Lamb, I'll tell thee:

He is called by thy name,
For he calls himself a Lamb.
He is meek, & he is mild
He became a little child:
I a child, & thou a lamb,
We are called by his name.
Little Lamb, God bless thee.
Little Lamb, God bless thee.

The Little Black Boy

My mother bore me in the southern wild,
And I am black, but O! my soul is white;
White as an angel is the English child,
But I am black, as if bereav'd of light.

My mother taught me underneath a tree,
And, sitting down before the heat of day
She took me on her lap and kissed me,
And pointing to the east began to say:

'Look on the rising sun: there God does live,
And gives his light, and gives his heat away;
And flowers and trees and beasts and men receive
Comfort in morning, joy in the noon day.

'And we are put on earth a little space,
That we may learn to bear the beams of love;
And these black bodies and this sun-burnt face
Is but a cloud, and like a shady grove.

'For when our souls have learn'd the heat to bear,
The cloud will vanish; we shall hear his voice,
Saying: "Come out from the grove, my love & care,
And round my golden tent like lambs rejoice."'

Thus did my mother say, and kissed me;
And thus I say to little English boy:
When I from black and he from white cloud free
And round the tent of God like lambs we joy,

I'll shade him from the heat, till he can bear
To lean in joy upon our father's knee;
And then I'll stand and stroke his silver hair,
And be like him, and he will then love me.

The Blossom

Merry, Merry Sparrow,
Under leaves so green,
A happy Blossom
Sees you, swift as arrow
Seek your cradle narrow
Near my Bosom.

Pretty, Pretty Robin,
Under leaves so green,
A happy Blossom
Hears you sobbing, sobbing,
Pretty, Pretty Robin,
Near my Bosom.

The Chimney Sweeper

When my mother died I was very young,
And my father sold me while yet my tongue
Could scarcely cry "weep! 'weep! 'weep! 'weep!'
So your chimneys I sweep, & in soot I sleep.

There's little Tom Dacre, who cried when his head,
That curl'd like a lamb's back, was shav'd; so I said,
'Hush, Tom, never mind it, for when your head's bare,
You know that the soot cannot spoil your white hair.'

And so he was quiet, and that very night,
As Tom was asleeping, he had such a sight:
That thousands of sweepers, Dick, Joe, Ned, & Jack,
Were all of them lock'd up in coffins of black;

And by came an Angel who had a bright key,
And he open'd the coffins and set them all free;
Then down a green plain leaping, laughing, they run,
And wash in a river, and shine in the Sun.

Then naked & white, all their bags left behind,
They rise upon clouds, and sport in the wind;
And the Angel told Tom, if he'd be a good boy,
He'd have God for his father & never want joy.

And so Tom awoke; and we rose in the dark,
And got with our bags & our brushes to work.
Tho' the morning was cold, Tom was happy & warm;
So if all do their duty they need not fear harm.

The Little Boy Lost

'Father, father, where are you going?
O do not walk so fast.
Speak, father, speak to your little boy,
Or else I shall be lost.'

The night was dark, no father was there;
The child was wet with dew;
The mire was deep, & the child did weep,
And away the vapour flew.

The Little Boy Found

The little boy lost in the lonely fen,
Led by the wand'ring light,
Began to cry, but God ever nigh,
Appear'd like his father in white.
He kissed the child & by the hand led

And to his mother brought,
Who in sorrow pale, thro' the lonely dale,
Her little boy weeping sought.

Laughing Song

When the green woods laugh with the voice of joy,
And the dimpling stream runs laughing by;
When the air does laugh with our merry wit,
And the green hill laughs with the noise of it;

When the meadows laugh with lively green,
And the grasshopper laughs in the merry scene,
When Mary and Susan and Emily
With their sweet round mouths sing 'Ha, Ha, He!'

When the painted birds laugh in the shade
Where our table with cherries and nuts is spread,
Come live, & be merry and join with me,
To sing the sweet chorus of 'Ha, Ha, He!'

A Cradle Song

Sweet dreams, form a shade
O'er my lovely infant's head,
Sweet dreams of pleasant streams
By happy silent, moony beams.

Sweet sleep, with soft down
Weave thy brows an infant crown.
Sweet sleep, Angel mild,
Hover o'er my happy child.

Sweet smiles, in the night
Hover over my delight.
Sweet smiles, Mother's smiles,
All the livelong night beguiles.

Sweet moans, dovelike sighs,
Chase not slumber from thy eyes.
Sweet moans, sweeter smiles,
All the dovelike moans beguiles.
Sleep, sleep, happy child,

All creation slept and smil'd.
Sleep, sleep, happy sleep,
While o'er thee thy mother weep.

Sweet babe, in thy face
Holy image I can trace.
Sweet babe, once like thee
Thy Maker lay, and wept for me,

Wept for me, for thee, for all,
When he was an infant small.
Thou his image ever see,
Heavenly face that smiles on thee,

Smiles on thee, on me, on all,
Who became an infant small,
Infant smiles are his own smiles;
Heaven & earth to peace beguiles.

The Divine Image

To Mercy, Pity, Peace, and Love
All pray in their distress;
And to these virtues of delight
Return their thankfulness.

For Mercy, Pity, Peace, and Love
Is God our Father dear,
And Mercy, Pity, Peace, and Love
Is Man, his child and care.

For Mercy has a human heart,
Pity, a human face,
And Love, the human form divine,
And Peace the human dress.

Then every man, of every clime
That prays in his distress,
Prays to the human form divine.
Love, Mercy, Pity, Peace.

And all must love the human form
In heathen, turk, or Jew.
Where Mercy, Love, & Pity dwell
There God is dwelling too.

Holy Thursday

'Twas on a Holy Thursday, their innocent faces clean,
The children walking two & two, in red, & blue, & green;
Grey headed beadles walk'd before, with wands as white as snow,
Till into the high dome of Paul's they like Thames' waters flow.
O what a multitude they seem'd, these flowers of London town!
Seated in companies they sit with radiance all their own.
The hum of multitudes was there, but multitudes of lambs,
Thousands of little boys & girls raising their innocent hands.
Now like a mighty wind they raise to heaven the voice of song,
Or like harmonious thunderings the seats of heaven among.
Beneath them sit the aged men, wise guardians of the poor.
Then cherish pity, lest you drive an angel from your door.

Night

The sun descending in the west,
The evening star does shine;
The birds are silent in their nest,
And I must seek for mine.
The moon, like a flower
In heaven's high bower,
With silent delight
Sits and smiles on the night.

Farewell, green fields and happy groves,
Where flocks have took delight;
Where lambs have nibbled, silent moves
The feet of angels bright;
Unseen, they pour blessing,
And joy without ceasing,
On each bud and blossom
And each sleeping bosom.

They look in every thoughtless nest,
Where birds are covered warm;
They visit caves of every beast,

To keep them all from harm;
If they see any weeping
That should have been sleeping,
They pour sleep on their head
And sit down by their bed.

When wolves and tigers howl for prey,
They pitying stand and weep,
Seeking to drive their thirst away
And keep them from the sheep;
But if they rush dreadful,
The angels, most heedful,
Receive each mild spirit,
New worlds to inherit.

And there the lion's ruddy eyes
Shall flow with tears of gold,
And pitying the tender cries,
And walking round the fold,
Saying, 'Wrath by his meekness,
And, by his health, sickness,
Is driven away
From our immortal day.

'And now beside thee, bleating lamb,
I can lie down and sleep,
Or think on Him who bore thy name,
Graze after thee, and weep.
For, wash'd in life's river,
My bright mane for ever
Shall shine like the gold,
As I guard o'er the fold.'

Spring

Sound the Flute!
Now it's mute.
Birds delight
Day and Night;
Nightingale
In the dale,

Lark in Sky,—
Merrily,
Merrily, Merrily to welcome in the Year.
Little Boy
Full of joy,
Little Girl
Sweet and small;
Cock does crow,
So do you;
Merry voice,
Infant noise;
Merrily, Merrily to welcome in the Year.
Little Lamb
Here I am;
Come and lick
My white neck,
Let me pull
Your soft Wool,
Let me kiss
Your soft face;
Merrily, Merrily we welcome in the Year.

Nurse's Song

When the voices of children are heard on the green
And laughing is heard on the hill,
My heart is at rest within my breast
And every thing else is still.

'Then come home, my children, the sun is gone down
And the dews of night arise;
Come, come, leave off play, and let us away
Till the morning appears in the skies.'

'No, no, let us play, for it is yet day
And we cannot go to sleep;
Besides, in the sky the little birds fly
And the hills are all cover'd with sheep.'
'Well, well, go & play till the light fades away
And then go home to bed.'

The little ones leaped, & shouted & laugh'd,
And all the hills ecchoed.

Infant Joy

'I have no name;
I am but two days old.'
What shall I call thee?
'I happy am,
Joy is my name.'
Sweet joy befall thee!

Pretty joy!
Sweet joy but two days old,
Sweet joy I call thee:
Thou dost smile,
I sing the while,
Sweet joy befall thee.

A Dream

Once a dream did weave a shade
O'er my angel-guarded bed,
That an Emmet lost its way
Where on grass methought I lay.

Troubled, 'wilder'd and forlorn,
Dark, benighted, travel-worn,
Over many a tangled spray
All heart-broke, I heard her say:

'O my children! do they cry?
Do they hear their father sigh?
Now they look abroad to see,
Now return and weep for me.'

Pitying, I drop'd a tear;
But I saw a glow-worm near,
Who replied: 'What wailing wight
Calls the watchman of the night?
'I am set to light the ground,
While the beetle goes his round:

Follow now the beetle's hum;
Little wanderer, hie thee home.'

On Another's Sorrow

Can I see another's woe,
And not be in sorrow too?
Can I see another's grief,
And not seek for kind relief?

Can I see a falling tear,
And not feel my sorrow's share?
Can a father see his child
Weep, nor be with sorrow fill'd?

Can a mother sit and hear
An infant groan, an infant fear?
No, no, never can it be,
Never, never can it be!

And can He who smiles on all
Hear the wren with sorrows small,
Hear the small bird's grief & care,
Hear the woes that infants bear,

And not sit beside the nest,
Pouring pity in their breast;
And not sit the cradle near,
Weeping tear on infant's tear;

And not sit both night & day,
Wiping all our tears away?
O no, never can it be,
Never, never can it be!

He doth give his joy to all;
He becomes an infant small;
He becomes a man of woe;
He doth feel the sorrow too.

Think not thou canst sigh a sigh
And thy maker is not by;
Think not thou canst weep a tear
And thy maker is not near.

O, he gives to us his joy
That our grief he may destroy;
Till our grief is fled & gone
He doth sit by us and moan.

SONGS OF EXPERIENCE

Introduction

Hear the voice of the Bard!
Who Present, Past & Future sees,
Whose ears have heard
The Holy Word
That walk'd among the ancient trees,

Calling the lapsed Soul,
And weeping in the evening dew,
That might controll
The starry pole,
And fallen, fallen light renew!

'O Earth, O Earth, return!
Arise from out the dewy grass;
Night is worn,
And the morn
Rises from the slumberous mass.

'Turn away no more.
Why wilt thou turn away?
The starry floor,
The wat'ry shore,
Is giv'n thee till the break of day.'

Earth's Answer

Earth rais'd up her head
From the darkness dread & drear.
Her light fled:
Stony dread!
And her locks cover'd with grey despair.

'Prison'd on wat'ry shore
Starry jealousy does keep my den
Cold and hoar
Weeping o'er
I hear the father of the ancient men.

'Selfish father of men!
Cruel, jealous, selfish fear!
Can delight,
Chain'd in night,
The virgins of youth and morning bear?

'Does spring hide its joy
When buds and blossoms grow?
Does the sower
Sow by night?
Or the ploughman in darkness plow?

'Break this heavy chain
That does freeze my bones around.
Selfish! vain!
Eternal bane!
That free Love with bondage bound.'

The Clod & The Pebble

'Love seeketh not itself to please,
Nor for itself hath any care,
But for another gives its ease,
And builds a Heaven in Hell's despair.'

So sang a little Clod of Clay
Trodden with the cattle's feet;
But a Pebble of the brook
Warbled out these metres meet:

'Love seeketh only Self to please,
To bind another to Its delight;
Joys in another's loss of ease,
And builds a Hell in Heaven's despite.'

Holy Thursday

Is this a holy thing to see
In a rich and fruitful land,
Babes reduced to misery,
Fed with cold and usurous hand?

Is that trembling cry a song?
Can it be a song of joy?
And so many children poor?
It is a land of poverty!

And their sun does never shine,
And their fields are bleak & bare,
And their ways are fill'd with thorns;
It is eternal winter there.

For where-e'r the sun does shine,
And where-e'r the rain does fall,
Babe can never hunger there,
Nor poverty the mind appall.

The Little Girl Lost

In futurity
I prophetic see
That the earth from sleep
(Grave the sentence deep)

Shall arise, and seek
For her maker meek,
And the desart wild
Become a garden mild.

In the southern clime,
Where the summer's prime
Never fades away,
Lovely Lyca lay.

Seven summers old
Lovely Lyca told.
She had wandered long,
Hearing wild birds' song.

'Sweet sleep, come to me
Underneath this tree.
Do father, mother, weep,
Where can Lyca sleep?

'Lost in desart wild
Is your little child.
How can Lyca sleep
If her mother weep?

'If her heart does ake,
Then let Lyca wake;
If my mother sleep,
Lyca shall not weep.

'Frowning, frowning night,
O'er this desart bright
Let thy moon arise,
While I close my eyes.'

Sleeping Lyca lay,
While the beasts of prey,
Come from caverns deep,
View'd the maid asleep.

The kingly lion stood
And the virgin view'd;
Then he gambol'd round
O'er the hallow'd ground.

Leopards, tygers play
Round her as she lay,
While the lion old
Bow'd his mane of gold,

And her bosom lick,
And upon her neck
From his eyes of flame
Ruby tears there came;

While the lioness
Loos'd her slender dress,
And naked they convey'd
To caves the sleeping maid.

The Little Girl Found

All the night in woe
Lyca's parents go
Over vallies deep,
While the desarts weep.

Tired and woe-begone,
Hoarse with making moan,
Arm in arm, seven days
They trac'd the desart ways.

Seven nights they sleep
Among shadows deep,
And dream they see their child
Starv'd in desert wild.

Pale thro' pathless ways
The fancied image strays,
Famish'd, weeping, weak,
With hollow piteous shriek.

Rising from unrest,
The trembling woman prest
With feet of weary woe;
She could no further go.

In his arms he bore
Her, arm'd with sorrow sore,
Till before their way
A couching lion lay.

Turning back was vain;
Soon his heavy mane
Bore them to the ground;
Then he stalk'd around,

Smelling to his prey.
But their fears allay
When he licks their hands,
And silent by them stands.

They look upon his eyes
Fill'd with deep surprise,
And wondering behold
A Spirit arm'd in gold.

On his head a crown,
On his shoulders down
Flow'd his golden hair.
Gone was all their care.

'Follow me,' he said;
'Weep not for the maid;
In my palace deep,
Lyca lies asleep.'

Then they followed
Where the vision led,
And saw their sleeping child
Among tigers wild.

To this day they dwell
In a lonely dell,
Nor fear the wolvish howl
Nor the lion's growl.

The Chimney Sweeper

A little black thing among the snow,
Crying 'weep! weep!' in notes of woe!
'Where are thy father & mother, say?'
'They are both gone up to the church to pray.

'Because I was happy upon the heath,
And smil'd among the winter's snow,
They clothed me in the clothes of death,
And taught me to sing the notes of woe.

'And because I am happy & dance & sing,
They think they have done me no injury;
And are gone to praise God & his Priest & King,
Who made up a heaven of our misery.'

Nurse's Song

When the voices of children are heard on the green,
And whisp'rings are in the dale,
The days of my youth rise fresh in my mind,
My face turns green and pale.

Then come home my children, the sun is gone down
And the dews of night arise;
Your spring & your day are wasted in play,
And your winter and night in disguise.

The Sick Rose

O Rose, thou art sick.
The invisible worm,
That flies in the night
In the howling storm,

Has found out thy bed
Of crimson joy;
And his dark secret love
Does thy life destroy.

The Fly

Little Fly,
Thy summer's play
My thoughtless hand
Has brush'd away.

Am not I
A fly like thee?
Or art not thou
A man like me?

For I dance
And drink, & sing
Till some blind hand
Shall brush my wing.

If thought is life
And strength & breath,
And the want
Of thought is death,

Then am I
A happy fly,
If I live
Or if I die.

The Angel

I Dreamt a Dream! what can it mean?
And that I was a maiden Queen,
Guarded by an Angel mild:
Witless woe was ne'er beguil'd!

And I wept both night and day,
And he wip'd my tears away,
And I wept both day and night,
And hid from him my heart's delight.

So he took his wings; and fled;
Then the morn blush'd rosy red;
I dried my tears, & arm'd my fears
With ten thousand shields and spears.

Soon my Angel came again;
I was arm'd, he came in vain;
For the time of youth was fled
And grey hairs were on my head.

The Tyger

Tyger, Tyger, burning bright
In the forests of the night,
What immortal hand or eye
Could frame thy fearful symmetry?

In what distant deeps or skies
Burnt the fire of thine eyes?
On what wings dare he aspire?
What the hand dare sieze the fire?

And what shoulder, & what art,
Could twist the sinews of thy heart?
And when thy heart began to beat,
What dread hand? & what dread feet?
What the hammer? what the chain?
In what furnace was thy brain?
What the anvil? what dread grasp
Dare its deadly terrors clasp?

When the stars threw down their spears
And water'd heaven with their tears,
Did he smile his work to see?
Did he who made the Lamb make thee?

Tyger, Tyger, burning bright
In the forests of the night,
What immortal hand or eye
Dare frame thy fearful symmetry?

My Pretty Rose Tree

A flower was offer'd to me,
Such a flower as May never bore;
But I said, 'I've a Pretty Rose-tree,
And I passed the sweet flower o'er.

Then I went to my Pretty rose-tree,
To tend her by day and by night;
But my Rose turned away with jealousy,
And her thorns were my only delight.

Ah! Sun-flower

Ah, Sun-flower! weary of time,
Who countest the steps of the Sun,
Seeking after that sweet golden clime
Where the traveller's journey is done;

Where the Youth pined away with desire,
And the pale Virgin shrouded in snow,
Arise from their graves and aspire
Where my Sun-flower wishes to go.

The Lilly

The modest Rose puts forth a thorn,
The humble Sheep a threat'ning horn;
While the Lilly white shall in Love delight,
Nor a thorn nor a threat stain her beauty bright.

The Garden of Love

I went to the Garden of Love,
And saw what I never had seen:
A Chapel was built in the midst,
Where I used to play on the green.
And the gates of this Chapel were shut,
And 'Thou shalt not' writ over the door;
So I turn'd to the Garden of Love
That so many sweet flowers bore,
And I saw it was filled with graves,
And tomb-stones where flowers should be;
And Priests in black gowns were walking their rounds,
And binding with briars my joys & desires.

The Little Vagabond

Dear Mother, dear Mother, the Church is cold,
But the Ale-house is healthy, & pleasant, & warm;
Besides I can tell where I am used well,
Such usage in heaven will never do well.

But if at the Church they would give us some Ale,
And a pleasant fire our souls to regale,
We'd sing and we'd pray all the live-long day,
Nor ever once wish from the Church to stray.

Then the Parson might preach, & drink, & sing,
And we'd be as happy as birds in the spring;
And modest dame Lurch, who is always at Church,
Would not have bandy children nor fasting nor birch.

And God, like a father rejoicing to see
His children as pleasant and happy as he,
Would have no more quarrel with the Devil or the Barrel,
But kiss him & give him both drink and apparel.

London

I wander thro' each charter'd street
Near where the charter'd Thames does flow,
And mark in every face I meet
Marks of weakness, marks of woe.

In every cry of every Man,
In every infant's cry of fear,
In every voice, in every ban,
The mind-forg'd manacles I hear:

How the chimney-sweeper's cry
Every black'ning church appalls,
And the hapless Soldier's sigh
Runs in blood down Palace walls;

But most, thro' midnight streets I hear
How the youthful Harlot's curse
Blasts the new born infant's tear,
And blights with plagues the Marriage hearse.

The Human Abstract

Pity would be no more
If we did not make somebody Poor;
And Mercy no more could be
If all were as happy as we;

And mutual fear brings peace,
Till the selfish loves increase.
Then Cruelty knits a snare
And spreads his baits with care.

He sits down with holy fears,
And waters the ground with tears;
Then Humility takes its root
Underneath his foot.

Soon spreads the dismal shade
Of Mystery over his head,
And the Catterpiller and Fly
Feed on the Mystery.

And it bears the fruit of Deceit,
Ruddy and sweet to eat,
And the Raven his nest has made
In its thickest shade.

The Gods of the earth and sea
Sought thro' nature to find this Tree;
But their search was all in vain:
There grows one in the human Brain.

Infant Sorrow

My mother groan'd, my father wept;
Into the dangerous world I leapt,
Helpless, naked, piping loud,
Like a fiend hid in a cloud.

Struggling in my father's hands,
Striving against my swadling bands,
Bound and weary, I thought best
To sulk upon my mother's breast.

A Poison Tree

I was angry with my friend;
I told my wrath, my wrath did end.
I was angry with my foe;
I told it not, my wrath did grow.

And I water'd it in fears,
Night & morning with my tears;
And I sunned it with smiles,
And with soft deceitful wiles.

And it grew both day and night,
Till it bore an apple bright;
And my foe beheld it shine,
And he knew that it was mine,
And into my garden stole
When the night had veil'd the pole.
In the morning glad I see
My foe outstretch'd beneath the tree.

A Little Boy Lost

'Nought loves another as itself,
Nor venerates another so,

Nor is it possible to Thought
A greater than itself to know.

'And Father, how can I love you
Or any of my brothers more?
I love you like the little bird
That picks up crumbs around the door.'

The Priest sat by and heard the child;
In trembling zeal he seiz'd his hair;
He led him by his little coat;
And all admir'd his Priestly care.

And standing on the altar high,
'Lo, what a fiend is here!' said he,
'One who sets reason up for judge
Of our most holy Mystery.'

The weeping child could not be heard,
The weeping parents wept in vain;
They strip'd him to his little shirt,
And bound him in an iron chain,

And burn'd him in a holy place
Where many had been burn'd before.
The weeping parents wept in vain.
Are such things done on Albion's shore?

A Little Girl Lost

Children of the future Age,
Reading this indignant page,
Know that in a former time
Love! sweet love! was thought a crime.
In the Age of Gold,
Free from winter's cold,
Youth and maiden bright,
To the holy light,
Naked in the sunny beams delight.

Once a youthful pair,
Fill'd with softest care,
Met in garden bright
Where the holy light
Had just remov'd the curtains of the night.

There in rising day,
On the grass they play;
Parents were afar,
Strangers came not near,
And the maiden soon forgot her fear.

Tired with kisses sweet,
They agree to meet
When the silent sleep
Waves o'er heaven's deep,
And the weary tired wanderers weep.

To her father white
Came the maiden bright;
But his loving look,
Like the holy book,
All her tender limbs with terror shook.

'Ona! pale and weak!
To thy father speak.
O the trembling fear!
O the dismal care!
That shakes the blossoms of my hoary hair.'

To Tirzah

Whate'er is Born of Mortal Birth
Must be consumed with the Earth
To rise from Generation free.
Then what have I to do with thee?
The Sexes sprung from Shame & Pride,
Blow'd in the morn, in evening died;
But Mercy chang'd Death into Sleep;
The Sexes rose to work & weep.

Thou Mother of my Mortal part
With cruelty didst mould my Heart,
And with false self-deceiving tears
Didst bind my Nostrils, Eyes & Ears;

Didst close my Tongue in senseless clay,
And me to Mortal Life betray.
The Death of Jesus set me free:
Then what have I to do with thee?

The School Boy

I love to rise in a summer morn,
When the birds sing on every tree;
The distant huntsman winds his horn,
And the sky-lark sings with me.
O! what sweet company

But to go to school in a summer morn,
O! it drives all joy away;
Under a cruel eye outworn
The little ones spend the day
In sighing and dismay.

Ah! then at times I drooping sit,
And spend many an anxious hour;
Nor in my book can I take delight,
Nor sit in learning's bower,
Worn thro' with the dreary shower.

How can the bird that is born for joy
Sit in a cage and sing?
How can a child when fears annoy
But droop his tender wing,
And forget his youthful spring?

O! father & mother, if buds are nip'd,
And blossoms blown away,
And if the tender plants are strip'd
Of their joy in the springing day
By sorrow and care's dismay,

How shall the summer arise in joy,
Or the summer fruits appear?
Or how shall we gather what griefs destroy,
Or bless the mellowing year
When the blasts of winter appear?

The Voice of the Ancient Bard

Youth of delight, come hither,
And see the opening morn,
Image of truth newborn.
Doubt is fled, & clouds of reason,
Dark disputes & artful teazing.
Folly is an endless maze,
Tangled roots perplex her ways:
How many have fallen there!
They stumble all night over bones of the dead,
And feel they know not what but care,
And wish to lead others when they should be led.

A Divine Image

Cruelty has a Human Heart,
And Jealousy a Human Face;
Terror the Human form Divine,
And Secrecy the Human Dress.

The Human Dress is forged Iron,
The Human Form a fiery Forge,
The Human Face a Furnace seal'd,
The Human Heart its hungry Gorge.

BLAKE'S NOTEBOOK
(C. 1791-3)

*

I told my love I told my love
I told her all my heart,
Trembling, cold in ghastly fears
Ah she doth depart

Soon as she was gone from me
A traveller came by
Silently, invisibly
O, was no deny.

*

I saw a chapel all of gold
That none did dare to enter in;
And many weeping stood without,
Weeping, mourning, worshipping.

I saw a serpent rise between
The white pillars of the door.
And he forc'd & forc'd & forc'd —
Down the golden hinges tore,

And along the pavement sweet,
Set with pearls & rubies bright,
All his slimy length he drew,
Till upon the altar white

Vomiting his poison out
On the bread & on the wine.
So I turn'd into a sty,
And laid me down among the swine.

*

I asked a thief to steal me a peach;
He turned up his eyes.
I ask'd a lithe lady to lie her down;
Holy & meek she cries.

As soon as I went
An angel came;
He wink'd at the thief
And smil'd at the dame,

And without one word said
Had a peach from the tree,
And still as a maid
Enjoy'd the lady.

*

I heard an Angel singing
When the day was springing,
'Mercy, Pity, Peace,
Is the world's release.'

Thus he sung all day
Over the new mown hay,

Till the sun went down
And haycocks looked brown.

I heard a Devil curse
Over the heath & the furze,
'Mercy could be no more
If there was nobody poor;

'And pity no more could be
If all were as happy as we.'
At his curse the sun went down,
And the heavens gave a frown.

Down pour'd the heavy rain
Over the new-reap'd grain;
And Miserie's increase
Is Mercy, Pity, Peace.

A Cradle Song

Sleep, Sleep, beauty bright,
Dreaming o'er the joys of night.
Sleep, Sleep; in thy sleep
Little sorrows sit & weep.

Sweet Babe, in thy face
Soft desires I can trace,
Secret joys & secret smiles,
Little pretty infant wiles.

As thy softest limbs I feel,
Smiles as of the morning steal
O'er thy cheek, & o'er thy breast
Where thy little heart doth rest.

O, the cunning wiles that creep
In thy little heart asleep!
When thy little heart doth wake,
Then the dreadful lightnings break

From thy cheek & from thy eye,
O'er the youthful harvests nigh.
Infant wiles & infant smiles
Heaven & Earth of peace beguiles.

*

I fear'd the fury of my wind
Would blight all blossoms fair and true,
And my sun it shin'd & shin'd,
And my wind it never blew.

But a blossom fair or true
Was not found on any tree;
For all blossoms grew & grew
Fruitless, false, tho' fair to see.

*

Silent, Silent Night,
Quench the holy light
Of thy torches bright;

For, possess'd of Day,
Thousand spirits stray
That sweet joys betray.

Why should joys be sweet
Used with deceit,
Nor with sorrows meet?

But an honest joy
Does itself destroy
For a harlot coy.

*

O Lapwing, thou fliest around the heath
Nor seest the net that is spread beneath.
Why dost thou not fly among the corn fields?
They cannot spread nets where a harvest yields.

To Nobodaddy

Why art thou silent & invisible,
Father of Jealousy?
Why dost thou hide thyself in clouds
From every searching Eye?

Why darkness & obscurity
In all thy words & laws,
That none dare eat the fruit but from
The wily serpent's jaws?

Or is it because Secrecy
Gains females' loud applause?

*

Love to faults is always blind,
Always is to joy inclin'd,
Lawless, wing'd & unconfin'd,
And breaks all chains from every mind.

Deceit to secrecy confin'd,
Lawful, cautious & refin'd,
To every thing but interest blind,
And forges fetters for the mind.

*

The sword sung on the barren heath,
The sickle in the fruitful field;
The sword he sung a song of death,
But could not make the sickle yield.

*

Abstinence sows sand all over
The ruddy limbs & flowing hair;
But Desire Gratified
Plants fruits of life & beauty there.

Eternity

He who binds to himself a joy
Does the winged life destroy;
But he who kisses the joy as it flies
Lives in eternity's sun rise.

Riches

The countless gold of a merry heart,
The rubies & pearls of a loving eye,
The indolent never can bring to the mart,
Nor the secret hoard up in his treasury.

*

The look of love alarms
Because' tis fill'd with fire;
But the look of soft deceit
Shall win the lover's hire.

Motto to the Songs of Innocence & of Experience

The Good are attracted by Men's perceptions,
And think not for themselves,
Till Experience teaches them to catch
And to Cage the Fairies & Elves.

And then the Knave begins to snarl,
And the Hypocrite to howl,
And all his good Friends show their private ends,
And the Eagle is known from the Owl.

THE BOOK OF THEL

PLATE 1

I

The daughters of Mne Seraphim led round their sunny flocks,
All but the youngest. She in paleness sought the secret air,
To fade away like morning beauty from her mortal day,
Down by the river of Adona her soft voice is heard,
And thus her gentle lamentation falls like morning dew:
'O life of this our spring! why fades the lotus of the water?
Why fade these children of the spring, born but to smile & fall?
Ah! Thel is like a wat'ry bow, and like a parting cloud,
Like a reflection in a glass, like shadows in the water,
Like dreams of infants, like a smile upon an infant's face;
Like the dove's voice, like transient day, like music in the air.
Ah! gentle may I lay me down, and gentle rest my head,
And gentle sleep the sleep of death, and gentle hear the voice
Of him that walketh in the garden in the evening time.'
The Lilly of the Valley, breathing in the humble grass,
Answer'd the lovely maid, and said: 'I am a wat'ry weed,

And I am very small, and love to dwell in lowly vales;
So weak the gilded butterfly scarce perches on my head;
Yet I am visited from heaven, and he that smiles on all
Walks in the valley, and each morn over me spreads his hand,
Saying, "Rejoice, thou humble grass, thou new-born lilly flower,
Thou gentle maid of silent valleys and of modest brooks;
For thou shalt be clothed in light, and fed with morning manna,
Till summer's heat melts thee beside the fountains and the springs
To flourish in eternal vales." Then why should Thel complain?

PLATE 2

Why should the mistress of the vales of Har utter a sigh?'
She ceas'd, & smil'd in tears, then sat down in her silver shrine.
Thel answer'd: 'O thou little virgin of the peaceful valley,
Giving to those that cannot crave, the voiceless, the o'erfired;
Thy breath doth nourish the innocent lamb, he smells thy milky garments,
He crops thy flowers while thou sittest smiling in his face,
Wiping his mild and meekin mouth from all contagious taints.
Thy wine doth purify the golden honey; thy perfume,
Which thou dost scatter on every little blade of grass that springs,
Revives the milked cow, & tames the fire-breathing steed.
But Thel is like a faint cloud kindled at the rising sun:
I vanish from my pearly throne, and who shall find my place?'
'Queen of the vales,' the Lilly answer'd, 'ask the tender cloud,
And it shall tell thee why it glitters in the morning sky,
And why it scatters its bright beauty thro' the humid air.
Descend, O little cloud, & hover before the eyes of Thel.'
The Cloud descended, and the Lilly bow'd her modest head,
And went to mind her numerous charge among the verdant grass.

PLATE 3 **II**

'O little Cloud,' the virgin said, 'I charge thee tell to me
Why thou complainest not when in one hour thou fade away;
Then we shall seek thee, but not find. Ah! Thel is like to thee:
I pass away: yet I complain, and no one hears my voice.'
The Cloud then show'd his golden head, & his bright form emerg'd,
Hovering and glittering on the air before the face of Thel:
'O virgin, know'st thou not? Our steeds drink of the golden springs
Where Luvah doth renew his horses. Look'st thou on my youth,
And fearest thou, because I vanish and am seen no more,
Nothing remains? O maid, I tell thee, when I pass away
It is to tenfold life, to love, to peace, and raptures holy.
Unseen descending, weigh my light wings upon balmy flowers,
And court the faireyed dew to take me to her shining tent.
The weeping virgin, trembling kneels before the risen sun,
Till we arise link'd in a golden band and never part,
But walk united, bearing food to all our tender flowers.'
'Dost thou, O little Cloud? I fear that I am not like thee'
For I walk thro' the vales of Har, and smell the sweetest flowers,
But I feed not the little flowers. I hear the warbling birds,
But I feed not the warbling birds; they fly and seek their food.
But Thel delights in these no more, because I fade away;
And all shall say, "Without a use this shining woman liv'd,
Or did she only live to be at death the food of worms?"'
The Cloud reclin'd upon his airy throne and answer'd thus:
'Then if thou art the food of worms, O virgin of the skies,
How great thy use, how great thy blessing! Every thing that lives
Lives not alone, nor for itself. Fear not, and I will call
The weak worm from its lowly bed, and thou shalt hear its voice.
Come forth, worm of the silent valley, to thy pensive queen.'
The helpless worm arose, and sat upon the Lilly's leaf,
And the bright Cloud sail'd on, to find his partner in the vale.

PLATE 4 **III**

Then Thel astonish'd view'd the Worm upon its dewy bed:
'Art thou a Worm? Image of weakness, art thou but a Worm?
I see thee like an infant wrapped in the Lilly's leaf.
Ah, weep not, little voice, thou canst not speak, but thou canst weep.
Is this a Worm? I see thee lay helpless and naked, weeping,
And none to answer, none to cherish thee with mother's smiles.'
The Clod of Clay heard the Worm's voice, & rais'd her pitying head;
She bow'd over the weeping infant, and her life exhal'd
In milky fondness; then on Thel she fix'd her humble eyes.
'O beauty of the vales of Har, we live not for ourselves.
Thou seest me the meanest thing, and so I am indeed.
My bosom of itself is cold, and of itself is dark,

PLATE 5

But he that loves the lowly, pours his oil upon my head,
And kisses me, and binds his nuptial bands around my breast,
And says: "Thou mother of my children, I have loved thee,
And I have given thee a crown that none can take away."
But how this is, sweet maid, I know not, and I cannot know;
I ponder, and I cannot ponder; yet I live and love.'
The daughter of beauty wip'd her pitying tears with her white veil,
And said: 'Alas! I knew not this, and therefore did I weep.
That God would love a Worm I knew, and punish the evil foot
That wilful bruis'd its helpless form; but that he cherish'd it
With milk and oil I never knew, and therefore did I weep;
And I complain'd in the mild air, because I fade away,
And lay me down in thy cold bed, and leave my shining lot.'
'Queen of the vales,' the matron Clay answer'd, 'I heard thy sighs,
And all thy moans flew o'er my roof, but I have call'd them down.
Wilt thou, O Queen, enter my house? 'Tis given thee to enter
and to return; fear nothing; enter with thy virgin feet.'

PLATE 6

IV

The eternal gates' terrific porter lifted the northern bar.
Thel enter'd in & saw the secrets of the land unknown.
She saw the couches of the dead, & where the fibrous roots
Of every heart on earth infixes deep its restless twists:
A land of sorrows & of tears where never smile was seen.
She wander'd in the land of clouds thro' valleys dark, list'ning
Dolours and lamentations; waiting oft beside a dewy grave
She stood in silence, list'ning to the voices of the ground,
Till to her own graveplot she came, and there she sat down,
And heard this voice of sorrow breathed from the hollow pit.
'Why cannot the Ear be closed to its own destruction?
Or the glist'ning Eye to the poison of a smile?
Why are Eyelids stor'd with arrows ready drawn,
Where a thousand fighting men in ambush lie,
Or an Eye of gifts & graces show'ring fruits and coined gold?
Why a Tongue impress'd with honey from every wind?
Why an Ear, a whirlpool fierce to draw creations in?
Why a Nostril wide inhaling terror, trembling, & affright?
Why a tender curb upon the youthful burning boy?
Why a little curtain of flesh on the bed of our desire?'
The Virgin started from her seat with a shriek
Fled back unhinder'd till she came into the vales of Har.

Thel's Motto

Does the Eagle know what is in the pit,
Or wilt thou go ask the Mole?
Can Wisdom be put in a silver rod,
Or Love in a golden bowl?

THE MARRIAGE OF HEAVEN AND HELL

The Argument

PLATE 2

Rintrah roars, & shakes his fires in the burden'd air;
Hungry clouds swag on the deep.

Once meek, and in a perilous path,
The just man kept his course along
The vale of death.
Roses are planted where thorns grow,
And on the barren heath
Sing the honey bees.

Then the perilous path was planted;
And a river and a spring
On every cliff and tomb;
And on the bleached bones
Red clay brought forth;

Till the villain left the paths of ease,
To walk in perilous paths, and drive
The just man into barren climes.

Now the sneaking serpent walks
In mild humility,
And the just man rages in the wilds
Where lions roam.

Rintrah roars, & shakes his fires in the burden'd air;
Hungry clouds swag on the deep.

PLATE 3

As a new heaven is begun, and it is now thirty-three years since its advent, the Eternal Hell revives. And lo! Swedenborg is the Angel sitting at the tomb; his writings are the linen clothes folded up. Now is the dominion of Edom, & the return of Adam into Paradise; see Isaiah xxxiv & xxxv Chap.

Without Contraries is no progression. Attraction and Repulsion, Reason and Energy, Love and Hate, are necessary to Human existence.

From these contraries spring what the religious call Good & Evil. Good is the passive that obeys Reason. Evil is the active springing from Energy.

Good is Heaven. Evil is Hell.

The Voice of the Devil

PLATE 4

All Bibles or sacred codes have been the causes of the following Errors:

1. That Man has two real existing principles, Viz. a Body & a Soul.
2. That Energy, call'd Evil, is alone from the Body, & that Reason, call'd Good, is alone from the Soul.
3. That God will torment Man in Eternity for following his Energies.

But the following Contraries to these are True:

1. Man has no Body distinct from his Soul; for that call'd Body is a portion of Soul discern'd by the five Senses, the chief inlets of Soul in this age.
2. Energy is the only life and is from the Body, and Reason is the bound or outward circumference of Energy.
3. Energy is Eternal Delight.

PLATE 5-6

Those who restrain desire, do so because theirs is weak enough to be restrained; and the restrainer or reason usurps its place & governs the unwilling.

And being restrain'd it by degrees becomes passive, till it is only the shadow of desire.

The history of this is written in Paradise Lost, & the Governor or Reason is call'd Messiah.

And the original Archangel, or possessor of the command of the heavenly host, is call'd the Devil or Satan, and his children are call'd Sin & Death.

But in the Book of Job, Milton's Messiah is call'd Satan.

For this history has been adopted by both parties.

It indeed appear'd to Reason as if Desire was cast out; but the Devil's account is that the Messiah fell, & formed a heaven of what he stole from the Abyss.

This is shewn in the Gospel, where he prays to the Father to send the comforter, or Desire, that Reason may have Ideas to build on, the Jehovah of the Bible being no other than he who dwells in flaming fire. Know that after Christ's death, he became Jehovah.

But in Milton, the Father is Destiny, the Son a Ratio of the five senses, & the Holy-ghost Vacuum!

Note.The reason Milton wrote in fetters when he wrote of Angels & God, and at liberty when of Devils & Hell, is because he was a true Poet, and of the Devil's party without knowing it.

A Memorable Fancy

As I was walking among the fires of hell, delighted with the enjoyments of Genius, which to Angels look like torment and insanity, I collected some of their Proverbs, thinking that as the sayings used in a nation mark its character, so the Proverbs of Hell show the nature of Infernal wisdom better than any description of buildings or garments.

When I came home, on the abyss of the five senses, where a flat sided steep frowns over the present world, I saw a mighty Devil folded in black clouds hovering on the sides of the rock. With corroding fires he wrote the following sentence now perceived by the minds of men, & read by them on earth:

How do you know but ev'ry Bird that cuts the airy way
Is an immense world of delight, clos'd by your senses five?

Proverbs of Hell

In seed time learn, in harvest teach, in winter enjoy.
Drive your cart and your plough over the bones of the dead.
The road of excess leads to the palace of wisdom.
Prudence is a rich, ugly old maid courted by Incapacity.
He who desires but acts not breeds pestilence.
The cut worm forgives the plow.
Dip him in the river who loves water.
A fool sees not the same tree that a wise man sees.
He whose face gives no light shall never become a star.
Eternity is in love with the productions of time.
The busy bee has no time for sorrow.
The hours of folly are measur'd by the clock, but of wisdom no clock can measure.
All wholesome food is caught without a net or a trap.
Bring out number, weight & measure in a year of dearth.
No bird soars too high if he soars with his own wings.
A dead body revenges not injuries.
The most sublime act is to set another before you.

If the fool would persist in his folly he would become wise.

Folly is the cloke of knavery.

Shame is Pride's cloke.

PLATE 8

Prisons are built with stones of Law, Brothels with bricks of Religion.

The pride of the peacock is the glory of God.

The lust of the goat is the bounty of God.

The wrath of the lion is the wisdom of God.

The nakedness of woman is the work of God.

Excess of sorrow laughs. Excess of joy weeps.

The roaring of lions, the howling of wolves, the raging of the stormy sea, and the destructive sword are portions of eternity too great for the eye of man.

The fox condemns the trap, not himself.

Joys impregnate. Sorrows bring forth.

Let man wear the fell of the lion, woman the fleece of the sheep.

The bird a nest, the spider a web, man friendship.

The selfish, smiling fool & the sullen, frowning fool shall be both thought wise, that they may be a rod.

What is now proved was once only imagin'd.

The rat, the mouse, the fox, the rabbit watch the roots; the lion, the tyger, the horse, the elephant watch the fruits.

The cistern contains: the fountain overflows.

One thought fills immensity.

Always be ready to speak your mind, and a base man will avoid you.

Every thing possible to be believ'd is an image of truth.

The eagle never lost so much time as when he submitted to learn of the crow.

PLATE 9

The fox provides for himself, but God provides for the lion.

Think in the morning. Act in the noon. Eat in the evening. Sleep in the night.

He who has suffer'd you to impose on him, knows you.

As the plow follows words, so God rewards prayers.

The tygers of wrath are wiser than the horses of instruction.

Expect poison from the standing water.

You never know what is enough unless you know what is more than enough.

Listen to the fool's reproach! it is a kingly title!

The eyes of fire, the nostrils of air, the mouth of water, the beard of earth.

The weak in courage is strong in cunning.

The apple tree never asks the beech how he shall grow, nor the lion the horse how he shall take his prey.

The thankful receiver bears a plentiful harvest.

If others had not been foolish, we should be so.

The soul of sweet delight can never be defil'd.

When thou seest an Eagle, thou seest a portion of Genius; lift up thy head!

As the Catterpiller chooses the fairest leaves to lay her eggs on, so the priest lays his curse on the fairest joys.

To create a little flower is the labour of ages.

Damn braces. Bless relaxes.

The best wine is the oldest, the best water the newest.

Prayers plow not! Praises reap not!

Joys laugh not! Sorrows weep not!

PLATE 10

The head Sublime, the heart Pathos, the genitals Beauty, the hands & feet Proportion.

As the air to a bird or the sea to a fish, so is contempt to the contemptible.

The crow wish'd every thing was black, the owl that every thing was white.

Exuberance is Beauty.

If the lion was advised by the fox, he would be cunning.

Improvement makes straight roads; but the crooked roads without improvement are roads of Genius.

Sooner murder an infant in its cradle than nurse unacted desires.

Where man is not, nature is barren.

Truth can never be told so as to be understood, and not be believ'd.

Enough! or Too much

PLATE 11

The ancient Poets animated all sensible objects with Gods or Geniuses, calling them by the names and adorning them with the properties of woods, rivers, mountains, lakes, cities, nations, and whatever their enlarged and numerous senses could perceive.

And particularly they studied the genius of each city and country, placing it under its mental deity.

Till a system was formed, which some took advantage of & enslav'd the vulgar by attempting to realise or abstract the mental deities from their objects; thus began Priesthood.

Choosing forms of worship from poetic tales.

And at length they pronounc'd that the Gods had order'd such things.

Thus men forgot that All deities reside in the human breast.

A Memorable Fancy

PLATE 12-13

The Prophets Isaiah and Ezekiel dined with me, and I asked them how they dared so roundly to assert that God spake to them; and whether they did not think at the time that they would be misunderstood, & so be the cause of imposition.

Isaiah answer'd: 'I saw no God, nor heard any, in a finite organical perception; but my senses discover'd the infinite in every thing, and as I was then persuaded, & remain confirm'd, that the voice of honest indignation is the voice of God, I cared not for consequences, but wrote.'

Then I asked: 'Does a firm perswasion that a thing is so, make it so?'

He replied: 'All poets believe that it does, & in ages of imagination this firm perswasion removed mountains; but many are not capable of a firm perswasion of any thing.'

Then Ezekiel said: 'The philosophy of the east taught the first principles of human perception. Some nations held one principle for the origin, & some another. We of Israel taught that the Poetic Genius (as you now call it) was the first principle and all the others merely derivative, which was the cause of our despising the Priests & Philosophers of other countries, and prophecying that all Gods would at last be proved to originate in ours & to be the tributaries of the Poetic Genius. It was this that our great poet, King David, desired so fervently & invokes so patheticly, saying by this he conquers enemies & governs kingdoms. And we so loved our God, that we cursed in his name all the deities of surrounding nations, and asserted that they had rebelled. From these opinions the vulgar came to think that all nations would at last be subject to the Jews.'

'This,' said he, 'like all firm perswasions, is come to pass; for all nations believe the Jews' code and worship the Jews' god, and what greater subjection can be?'

I heard this with some wonder, & must confess my own conviction. After dinner I ask'd Isaiah to favour the world with his lost works; he said none of equal value was lost. Ezekiel said the same of his.

I also asked Isaiah what made him go naked and barefoot three years. He answer'd, 'The same that made our friend Diogenes the Grecian.'

I then asked Ezekiel why he ate dung, & lay so long on his right & left side? He answer'd, 'The desire of raising other men into a perception of the infinite. This the North American tribes practise, & is he honest who resists his genius or conscience only for the sake of present ease or gratification?'

PLATE 14

The ancient tradition that the world will be consumed in fire at the end of six thousand years is true, as I have heard from Hell.

For the cherub with his flaming sword is hereby commanded to leave his guard at tree of life; and when he does, the whole creation will be consumed & appear infinite and holy, whereas it now appears finite & corrupt.

This will come to pass by an improvement of sensual enjoyment.

But first the notion that man has a body distinct from his soul is to be expunged. This I shall do, by printing in the infernal method, by corrosives, which in Hell are salutary and medicinal, melting apparent surfaces away, and displaying the infinite which was hid.

If the doors of perception were cleansed everything would appear to man as it is, infinite.

For man has closed himself up till he sees all things thro' narrow chinks of his cavern.

A Memorable Fancy

PLATE 15

I was in a Printing house in Hell, & saw the method in which knowledge is transmitted from generation to generation.

In the first chamber was a Dragon-Man, clearing away the rubbish from a cave's mouth; within, a number of Dragons were hollowing the cave.

In the second chamber was a Viper folding round the rock & the cave, and others adorning it with gold, silver and precious stones.

In the third chamber was an Eagle with wings and feathers of air, he caused the inside of the cave to be infinite. Around were numbers of Eagle-like men who built palaces in the immense cliffs.

In the fourth chamber were Lions of flaming fire, raging around & melting the metals into living fluids.

In the fifth chamber were Unnam'd forms, which cast the metals into the expanse.

There they were receiv'd by Men who occupied the sixth chamber, and took the forms of books & were arranged in libraries.

PLATE 16-17

The Giants who formed this world into its sensual existence, and now seem to live in it in chains, are in truth the causes of its life & the sources of all activity; but the chains are the cunning of weak and tame minds which have power to resist energy. According to the proverb, the weak in courage is strong in cunning.

Thus one portion of being is the Prolific, the other the Devouring. To the Devourer it seems as if the producer was in his chains, but it is not so; he only takes portions of existence and fancies that the whole.

But the Prolific would cease to be Prolific unless the Devourer as a sea, received the excess of his delights.

Some will say, 'Is not God alone the Prolific? I answer, 'God only Acts and Is in existing beings or Men.'

These two classes of men are always upon earth, & they should be enemies: whoever tries to reconcile them seeks to destroy existence.

Religion is an endeavour to reconcile the two.

Note. Jesus Christ did not wish to unite, but to separate them, as in the Parable of sheep and goats! & he says, 'I came not to send Peace, but a Sword.'

Messiah or Satan or Tempter was formerly thought to be one of the Antediluvians who are our Energies.

A Memorable Fancy

An Angel came to me and said: 'O pitiable foolish young man! O horrible! O dreadful state! consider the hot burning dungeon thou art preparing for thyself to all eternity, to which thou art going in such career.'

I said: 'Perhaps you will be willing to show me my eternal lot, & we will contemplate together upon it, and see whether your lot or mine is most desirable.'

So he took me thro' a stable & thro' a church & down into the church vault, at the end of which was a mill. Thro' the mill we went, and came to a cave; down the winding cavern we groped our tedious way, till a void boundless as a nether sky appear'd beneath us, & we held by the roots of trees and hung over this immensity. But I said: 'If you please we will commit ourselves to this void, and see whether providence is here also; if you will not, I will.' But he answer'd: 'Do not presume, O young man, but as we here remain, behold thy lot which will soon appear when the darkness passes away.'

So I remain'd with him, sitting in the twisted root of an oak. He was suspended in a fungus, which hung with the head downward into the deep.

By degrees we beheld the infinite Abyss, fiery as the smoke of a burning city; beneath us at an immense distance, was the sun, black but shining. Round it were fiery tracks on which revolv'd vast spiders crawling after their prey, which flew or rather swum in the infinite deep, in the most terrific shapes of animals sprung from corruption; & the air was full of them & seem'd composed of them. These are Devils, and are called Powers of the air. I now asked my companion which was my eternal lot; he said: 'Between the black & white spiders.'

But now, from between the black & white spiders, a cloud and fire burst and rolled thro' the deep, blackning all beneath, so that the nether deep grew black as a sea, & rolled with a terrible noise. Beneath us was nothing now to be seen but a black tempest, till looking east between the clouds & the waves, we saw a cataract of blood mixed with fire, and not many stone's throw from us appear'd and sunk again the scaly fold of a monstrous serpent. At last, to the east, distant about three degrees, appear'd a fiery crest above the waves; slowly it reared like a ridge of golden rocks till we discover'd two globes of crimson fire, from which the sea fled away in clouds of smoke; and now we saw it was the head of Leviathan. His forehead was divided into streaks of green & purple like those on a tyger's forehead; soon we saw his mouth & red gills hang just above the raging foam, tinging the black deep with beams of blood, advancing toward us with all the fury of a spiritual existence.

My friend the Angel climb'd up from his station into the mill. I remain'd alone, & then this appearance was no more, but I found myself sitting on a pleasant bank beside a river, by moonlight, hearing a harper, who sung to the harp, & his theme was: 'The man who never alters his opinion is like standing water, & breeds reptiles of the mind.'

But I arose, and sought for the mill, & there I found my Angel, who surprised asked me how I escaped?

I answer'd: 'All that we saw was owing to your metaphysics; for when you ran away, I found myself on a bank by moonlight hearing a harper. But now we have seen my eternal lot, shall I show you yours?' He laugh'd at my proposal; but I by force suddenly caught him in my arms, & flew westerly thro' the night, till we were elevated above the earth's shadow. Then I flung myself with him directly into the body of the sun. Here I clothed myself in white, & taking in my hand Swedenborg's volumes, sunk from the glorious clime, and passed all the planets till we came to Saturn. Here I staid to rest, & then leap'd into the void between Saturn and the fixed stars.

'Here,' said I, 'is your lot, in this space, if space, it may be call'd.' Soon we saw the stable and the church, & I took him to the altar and open'd the Bible, and lo! it was a deep pit, into which I descended, driving the Angel before me. Soon we saw seven houses of brick; one we enter'd; in it were a number of monkeys, baboons, & all of that species, chain'd by the middle, grinning and snatching at one another, but withheld by the shortness of their chains. However I saw that they sometimes grew numerous, and then the weak were caught by the strong and, with a grinning aspect, first coupled with, & then devour'd, by plucking off first one limb and then another, till the body was left a helpless trunk. This after grinning and kissing it with seeming fondness they devour'd too; and here & there I saw one savourily picking the flesh off of his own tail. As the stench terribly annoy'd us both, we went into the mill, & I in my hand brought the skeleton of a body, which in the mill was Aristotle's Analytics.

So the Angel said: 'Thy phantasy has imposed upon me, &thou oughtest to be ashamed.'

I answer'd: 'We impose on one another, & it is but lost time to converse with you whose works are only Analytics.'

PLATES 21-22

I have always found that Angels have the vanity to speak of themselves as the only wise this they do with a confident insolence sprouting from systematic reasoning.

Thus Swedenborg boasts that what he writes is new, tho' it is only the Contents or Index of already publish'd books.

A man carried a monkey about for a shew, & because he was a little wiser than the monkey, grew vain; and conceiv'd himself as much wiser than seven men. It is so with Swedenborg; he shews the folly of churches & exposes hypocrites, till he imagines that all are religious, & himself the single one on earth that ever broke a net.

Now hear a plain fact: Swedenborg has not written one new truth. Now hear another: he has written all the old falsehoods.

And now hear the reason. He conversed with Angels who are all religious, & conversed not with Devils who all hate religion, for he was incapable thro' his conceited notions.

Thus Swedenborg's writings are a recapitulation of all superficial opinions, and an analysis of the more sublime—but no further.

Have now another plain fact: any man of mechanical talents may, from the writings of Paracelsus or Jacob Behmen, produce ten thousand volumes of equal value with Swedenborg's, and from those of Dante or Shakespear an infinite number.

But when he has done this, let him not say that he knows better than his master, for he only holds a candle in sunshine.

A Memorable Fancy

PLATES 22-24

Once I saw a Devil in a flame of fire, who arose before an Angel that sat on a cloud, and the Devil utter'd these words:

'The worship of God is: Honouring his gifts in other men, each according to his genius, and loving the greatest men best. Those who envy or calumniate great men hate God, for there is no other God.'

The Angel hearing this became almost blue; but mastering himself he grew yellow, & at last white pink, & smiling, and then replied:

'Thou Idolater, is not God One? & is not he visible in Jesus Christ? and has not Jesus Christ given his sanction to the law of ten commandments? and are not all other men fools, sinners, & nothings?'

The Devil answer'd: 'Bray a fool in a mortar with wheat, yet shall not his folly be beaten out of him. If Jesus Christ is the greatest man, you ought to love him in the greatest degree. Now hear how he has given his sanction to the law of ten commandments: did he not mock at the sabbath, and so mock the sabbath's God? murder those who were murder'd because of him? turn away the law from the woman taken in adultery? steal the labour of others to support him? bear false witness when he omitted making a defence before Pilate? covet when he pray'd for his disciples, and when he bid them shake off the dust of their feet against such as refused to lodge them? I tell you, no virtue can exist without breaking these ten commandments. Jesus was all virtue, and acted from impulse, not from rules.'

When he had so spoken, I beheld the Angel, who stretched out his arms embracing the flame of fire, & he was consumed and arose as Elijah.

Note. This Angel, who is now become a Devil, is my particular friend. We often read the Bible together in its infernal or diabolical sense, which the world shall have if they behave well.

I have also: The Bible of Hell, which the world shall have whether they will or no.

One Law for the Lion & Ox is Oppression.

A Song of Liberty

PLATES 25-27

1. The Eternal Female groan'd! it was heard over all the Earth.

2. Albion's coast is sick, silent; the American meadows faint!

3. Shadows of Prophecy shiver along by the lakes and the rivers, and mutter across the ocean: 'France, rend down thy dungeon!

4. Golden Spain, burst the barriers of old Rome!

5. Cast thy keys, O Rome, into the deep, down falling, even to eternity down falling,

6. And weep!'

7. In her trembling hands she took the new born terror, howling.

8. On those infinite mountains of light, now barr'd out by the Atlantic sea, the new born fire stood before the starry king!

9. Flag'd with grey brow'd snows and thunderous visages, the jealous wings wav'd over the deep.

10. The speary hand burned aloft, unbuckled was the shield; forth went the hand of jealousy among the flaming hair, and hurl'd the new born wonder thro' the starry night.

11. The fire, the fire, is falling!

12. Look up! look up! O citizen of London, enlarge thy countenance; O Jew, leave counting gold! return to thy oil and wine; O African! black African! (go winged thought, widen his forehead.)

13. The fiery limbs, the flaming hair shot like the sinking sun into the western sea.

14. Wak'd from his eternal sleep, the hoary element roaring fled away.

15. Down rush'd, beating his wings in vain, the jealous king; his grey brow'd councellors, thunderous warriors, curl'd veterans, among helms, and shields, and chariots, horses, elephants, banners, castles, slings and rocks.

16. Falling, rushing, ruining! buried in the ruins, on Urthona's dens.

17. All night beneath the ruins; then, their sullen flames faded, emerge round the gloomy king.

18. With thunder and fire, leading his starry hosts thro' the waste wilderness, he promulgates his ten commands, glancing his beamy eyelids over the deep in dark dismay,

19. Where the son of fire in his eastern cloud, while the morning plumes her golden breast,

20. Spurning the clouds written with curses, stamps the stony law to dust, loosing the eternal horses from the dens of night, crying:

'Empire is no more! and now the lion & wolf shall cease'.

Chorus

Let the Priests of the Raven of dawn no longer, in deadly black, with hoarse note curse the sons of joy. Nor his accepted brethren whom, tyrant, he calls free, lay the bound or build the roof. Nor pale religious letchery call that Virginity that wishes but acts not!

For everything that lives is Holy.

VISIONS OF THE DAUGHTERS OF ALBION

The Eye sees more than the Heart knows

The Argument

PLATE 3

'I loved Theotormon
And I was not ashamed;
I trembled in my virgin fears
And I hid in Leutha's vale.

'I plucked Leutha's flower,
And I rose up from the vale;
But the terrible thunders tore
My virgin mantle in twain.'

Visions

PLATE 1

Enslav'd, the Daughters of Albion weep: a trembling lamentation
Upon their mountains, in their valleys, sighs toward America.
For the soft soul of America, Oothoon, wander'd in woe
Along the vales of Leutha, seeking flowers to comfort her;
And thus she spoke to the bright Marigold of Leutha's vale:
'Art thou a flower? art thou a nymph? I see thee now a flower,
Now a nymph! I dare not pluck thee from thy dewy bed!'
The Golden nymph replied: 'Pluck thou my flower, Oothoon the mild.
Another flower shall spring, because the soul of sweet delight
Can never pass away.' She ceas'd, & clos'd her golden shrine.
Then Oothoon pluck'd the flower, saying, 'I pluck thee from thy bed,
Sweet flower, and put thee here to glow between my breasts,
And thus I turn my face to where my whole soul seeks.'
Over the waves she went in wing'd exulting swift delight,
And over Theotormon's reign took her impetuous course.
Bromion rent her with his thunders; on his stormy bed
Lay the faint maid, and soon her woes appall'd his thunders hoarse.
Bromion spoke: 'Behold this harlot here on Bromion's bed,
And let the jealous dolphins sport around the lovely maid.
Thy soft American plains are mine, and mine thy north & south.
Stampt with my signet are the swarthy children of the sun;
They are obedient, they resist not, they obey the scourge;
Their daughters worship terrors and obey the violent.

PLATE 2

Now thou maist marry Bromion's harlot, and protect the child
Of Bromion's rage, that Oothoon shall put forth in nine moons' time.'
Then storms rent Theotormon's limbs; he roll'd his waves around
And folded his black jealous waters round the adulterate pair.

Bound back to back in Bromion's caves, terror & meekness dwell.
At entrance Theotormon sits, wearing the threshold hard
With secret tears; beneath him sound like waves on a desart shore
The voice of slaves beneath the sun, and children bought with money,
That shiver in religious caves beneath the burning fires
Of lust, that belch incessant from the summits of the earth.
Oothoon weeps not; she cannot weep! her tears are locked up;
But she can howl incessant, writhing her soft snowy limbs
And calling Theotormon's Eagles to prey upon her flesh:
'I call with holy voice! kings of the sounding air,
Rend away this defiled bosom that I may reflect
The image of Theotormon on my pure transparent breast.'
The Eagles at her call descend and rend their bleeding prey:
Theotormon severely smiles; her soul reflects the smile,
As the clear spring muddied with feet of beasts grows pure & smiles.
The Daughters of Albion hear her woes, & echo back her sighs.
'Why does my Theotormon sit weeping upon the threshold,
And Oothoon hovers by his side, persuading him in vain?
I cry, Arise, O Theotormon, for the village dog
Barks at the breaking day, the nightingale has done lamenting,
The lark does rustle in the ripe corn, and the Eagle returns
From nightly prey and lifts his golden beak to the pure east,
Shaking the dust from his immortal pinions to awake
The sun that sleeps too long. Arise, my Theotormon, I am pure,
Because the night is gone that clos'd me in its deadly black"
They told me that the night & day were all that I could see;
They told me that I had five senses to enclose me up;
And they inclos'd my infinite brain into a narrow circle,
And sunk my heart into the Abyss, a red round globe, hot burning,
Till all from life I was obliterated and erased.
Instead of morn arises a bright shadow, like an eye
In the eastern cloud, instead of night a sickly charnelhouse,
That Theotormon hears me not! To him the night and morn
Are both alike: a night of sighs, a morning of fresh tears;

PLATE 3

And none but Bromion can hear my lamentations.
'With what sense is it that the chicken shuns the ravenous hawk?
With what sense does the tame pigeon measure out the expanse?
With what sense does the bee form cells? Have not the mouse & frog
Eyes and ears and sense of touch? yet are their habitations
And their pursuits as different as their forms and as their joys.
Ask the wild ass why he refuses burdens, and the meek camel
Why he loves man. Is it because of eye, ear, mouth, or skin,
Or breathing nostrils? No, for these the wolf and tyger have.
Ask the blind worm the secrets of the grave, and why her spires
Love to curl round the bones of death; and ask the rav'nous snake
Where she gets poison, & the wing'd eagle why he loves the sun;
And then tell me the thoughts of man that have been hid of old.
'Silent I hover all the night, and all day could be silent,
If Theotormon once would turn his loved eyes upon me.
How can I be defil'd when I reflect thy image pure?
Sweetest the fruit that the worm feeds on, & the soul prey'd on by woe,
The newwash'd lamb ting'd with the village smoke, & the bright swan
By the red earth of our immortal river. I bathe my wings,
And I am white and pure to hover round Theotormon's breast.'
Then Theotormon broke his silence, and he answered:
'Tell me what is the night or day to one o'erflow'd with woe?
Tell me what is a thought? & of what substance is it made?
Tell me what is a joy? in what gardens do joys grow?
And in what rivers swim the sorrows? and upon what mountains

PLATE 4

Wave shadows of discontent? and in what houses dwell the wretched,

Drunken with woe, forgotten and shut up from cold despair?
'Tell me where dwell the thoughts forgotten till thou call them forth?
Tell me where dwell the joys of old? & where the ancient loves,
And when will they renew again & the night of oblivion past?
That I might traverse times & spaces far remote and bring
Comforts into a present sorrow and a night of pain.
Where goest thou, O thought? to what remote land is thy flight?
If thou returnest to the present moment of affliction
Wilt thou bring comforts on thy wings, and dews and honey and balm,
Or poison from the desart wilds, from the eyes of the envier?'
Then Bromion said, and shook the cavern with his lamentation:
'Thou knowest that the ancient trees seen by thine eyes have fruit,
But knowest thou that trees and fruits flourish upon the earth
To gratify senses unknown? trees, beasts and birds unknown:
Unknown, not unperceiv'd, spread in the infinite microscope,
In places yet unvisited by the voyager, and in worlds
Over another kind of seas, and in atmospheres unknown?
Ah! are there other wars beside the wars of sword and fire?
And are there other sorrows beside the sorrows of poverty?
And are there other joys beside the joys of riches and ease?
And is there not one law for both the lion and the ox?
And is there not eternal fire, and eternal chains
To bind the phantoms of existence from eternal life?'
Then Oothoon waited silent all the day and all the night;

PLATE 5

But when the morn arose, her lamentation renew'd.
The Daughters of Albion hear her woes, & eccho back her sighs.
'O Urizen! Creator of men! mistaken Demon of heaven,
Thy joys are tears! thy labour vain to form men to thine image.
How can one joy absorb another? are not different joys
Holy, eternal, infinite? and each joy is a Love.
'Does not the great mouth laugh at a gift? & the narrow eyelids mock

At the labour that is above payment? and wilt thou take the ape
For thy counsellor? or the dog for a schoolmaster to thy children?
Does he who contemns poverty, and he who turns with abhorrence
From usury, feel the same passion, or are they moved alike?
How can the giver of gifts experience the delights of the merchant?
How the industrious citizen the pains of the husbandman?
How different far the fat fed hireling with hollow drum,
Who buys whole corn fields into wastes, and sings upon the heath:
How different their eye and ear! how different the world to them!
With what sense does the parson claim the labour of the farmer?
What are his nets & gins & traps, & how does he surround him
With cold floods of abstraction, and with forests of solitude,
To build him castle and high spires, where kings and priests may dwell,
Till she who burns with youth and knows no fixed lot, is bound
In spell of law to one she loathes? and must she drag the chain
Of life in weary lust? must chilling murderous thoughts obscure
The clear heaven of her eternal spring? to bear the wintry rage
Of a harsh terror, driv'n to madness, bound to hold a rod
Over her shrinking shoulders all the day, & all the night
To turn the wheel of false desire, and longings that wake her womb
To the abhorred birth of cherubs in the human form,
That live a pestilence & die a meteor & are no more;
Till the child dwell with one he hates, and do the deed he loathes,
And the impure scourge force his seed into its unripe birth
E'er yet his eyelids can behold the arrows of the day?
'Does the whale worship at thy footsteps as the hungry dog?
Or does he scent the mountain prey because his nostrils wide
Draw in the ocean? does his eye discern the flying cloud
As the raven's eye? or does he measures the expanse like the vulture?

Does the still spider view the cliffs where eagles hide their young?
Or does the fly rejoice because the harvest is brought in?
Does not the eagle scorn the earth & despise the treasures beneath?
But the mole knoweth what is there, & the worm shall tell it thee.
Does not the worm erect a pillar in the mouldering church yard,

PLATE 6

And a Palace of eternity in the jaws of the hungry grave?
Over his porch these words are written: "Take thy bliss, O Man!
And sweet shall be thy taste, & sweet thy infant joys renew!"
'Infancy, fearless, lustful, happy, nestling for delight
In laps of pleasures! Innocence, honest, open, seeking
The vigorous joys of morning light, open to virgin bliss!
Who taught thee modesty, subtil modesty, child of night & sleep?
When thou awakest, wilt thou dissemble thy secret joys,
Or wert thou awake when all this mystery was disclos'd?
Then com'st thou forth a modest virgin, knowing to dissemble,
With nets found under thy night pillow to catch virgin joy
And brand it with the name of whore, & sell it in the night,
In silence, ev'n without a whisper, and in seeming sleep.
Religious dreams and holy vespers light thy smoky fires;
Once were thy fires lighted by the eyes of honest morn.
And does my Theotormon seek this hypocrite modesty
This knowing, artful, secret, fearful, cautious, trembling hypocrite?
Then is Oothoon a whore indeed! and all the virgin joys
Of life are harlots, and Theotormon is a sick man's dream,
And Oothoon is the crafty slave of selfish holiness.
'But Oothoon is not so, a virgin fill'd with virgin fancies,
Open to joy and to delight wherever beauty appears:
If in the morning sun I find it, there my eyes are fix'd

PLATE 7

In happy copulation; if in evening mild, wearied with work,
Sit on a bank and draw the pleasures of this freeborn joy.
'The moment of desire! the moment of desire! The virgin
That pines for man shall awaken her womb to enormous joys
In the secret shadows of her chamber; the youth shut up from
The lustful joy shall forget to generate, & create an amorous image
In the shadows of his curtains and in the folds of his silent pillow.
Are not these the places of religion? the rewards of continence?
The selfenjoyings of selfdenial? Why dost thou seek religion?
Is it because acts are not lovely that thou seekest solitude,
Where the horrible darkness is impressed with reflections of desire?
'Father of Jealousy, be thou accursed from the earth!
Why hast thou taught my Theotormon this accursed thing?
Till beauty fades from off my shoulders, darken'd and cast out,
A solitary shadow wailing on the margin of non-entity.
'I cry, Love! Love! Love! happy, happy Love! free as the mountain wind!
Can that be Love, that drinks another as a sponge drinks water?
That clouds with jealousy his nights, with weepings all the day,
To spin a web of age around him, grey and hoary! dark!
Till his eyes sicken at the fruits that hangs before his sight?
Such is self-love that envise all! a creeping skeleton
With lamplike eyes watching around the frozen marriage bed.
'But silken nets and traps of adamant will Oothoon spread,
And catch for thee girls of mild silver, or of furious gold.
I'll lie beside thee on a bank, & view their wanton play
In lovely copulation, bliss on bliss with Theotormon.
Red as the rosy morning, lustful as the firstborn beam,
Oothoon shall view his dear delight, nor e'er with jealous cloud
Come in the heaven of generous love, nor selfish blightings bring.
'Does the sun walk in glorious raiment on the secret floor

PLATE 8

Where the cold miser spreads his gold? or does the bright cloud drop
On his stone threshold? does his eye behold the beam that brings
Expansion to the eye of pity? or will he bind himself
Beside the ox to thy hard furrow? does not that mild beam blot
The bat, the owl, the glowing tyger, and the king of night?
The seafowl takes the wintry blast for a cov'ring to her limbs,
And the wild snake the pestilence to adorn him with gems and gold;
And trees & birds & beasts & men behold their eternal joy.
Arise, you little glancing wings, and sing your infant joy!
Arise and drink your bliss, for everything that lives is holy!'
Thus every morning wails Oothoon; but Theotormon sits
Upon the morgin'd ocean conversing with shadows dire.
The Daughters of Albion hear her woes, & eccho back her sighs.

AMERICA

A Prophecy

Preludium

PLATE 1

The shadowy daughter of Urthona stood before red Orc,
When fourteen suns had faintly journey'd o'er his dark abode.
His food she brought in iron baskets, his drink in cups of iron.
Crown'd with a helmet & dark hair the nameless female stood;
A quiver with its burning stores, a bow like that of night
When pestilence is shot from heaven—no other arms she need;
Invulnerable tho' naked, save where clouds roll round her loins
Their awful folds in the dark air, Silent she stood as night;
For never from her iron tongue could voice or sound arise,
But dumb till that dread day when Orc assay'd his fierce embrace.

'Dark Virgin,' said the hairy Youth, 'thy father stern abhorr'd
Rivets my tenfold chains while still on high my spirit soars.
Sometimes an eagle screaming in the sky, sometimes a lion
Stalking upon the mountains, & sometimes a whale I lash
The raging fathomless abyss; anon a serpent folding
Around the pillars of Urthona, and round thy dark limbs,
On the Canadian wilds I fold; feeble my spirit folds,
For chain'd beneath I rend these caverns. When thou bringest food
I howl my joy, and my red eyes seek to behold thy face.
In vain! these clouds roll to & fro, & hide thee from my sight'.

PLATE 2

Silent as despairing love, and strong as jealousy,
The hairy shoulders rend the links; free are the wrists of fire;
Round the terrific loins he seiz'd the panting, struggling womb;
It joy'd. She put aside her clouds & smiled her first-born smile,
As when a block cloud shows its lightnings to the silent deep.
Soon as she saw the Terrible Boy, then burst the virgin cry:
'I know thee, I have found thee, and I will not let thee go:
Thou art the image of God who dwells in darkness of Africa,
And thou art fall'n to give me life in regions of dark death.
On my American plains I feel the struggling afflictions
Endur'd by roots that writhe their arms into the nether deep;
I see a serpent in Canada, who courts me to his love,
In Mexico an Eagle, and a Lion in Peru;
I see a Whale in the South-sea, drinking my soul away.
O what limbrending pains I feel; thy fire and my frost
Mingle in howling pains, in furrows by thy lightnings rent.
This is eternal death, and this the torment long foretold.'

A Prophecy

PLATE 3

The Guardian Prince of Albion burns in his nightly tent;
Sullen fires across the Atlantic glow to America's shore,
Piercing the souls of warlike men who rise in silent night.

Washington, Franklin, Paine & Warren, Gates, Hancock & Green
Meet on the coast glowing with blood from Albion's fiery Prince.
Washington spoke: 'Friends of America, look over the Atlantic sea;
A bended bow is lifted in heaven, & a heavy iron chain
Descends link by link, from Albion's cliffs across the sea to bind
Brothers & sons of America, till our faces pale and yellow,
Heads deprest voices weak, eyes downcast, hands work-bruis'd,
Feet bleeding on the sultry sands, and the furrows of the whip
Descend to generations that in future times forget.'
The strong voice ceas'd; for a terrible blast swept over the heaving sea.
The eastern cloud rent; on his cliffs stood Albion's wrathful Prince,
A dragon form, clashing his scales; at midnight he arose,
And flam'd red meteors round the land of Albion beneath.
His voice, his locks, his awful shoulders, and his glowing eyes

PLATE 4

Appear to the Americans upon the cloudy night.
Solemn heave the Atlantic waves between the gloomy nations,
Swelling, belching from its deeps red clouds & raging fires.
Albions is sick, America faints! enrag'd the Zenith grew.
As human blood shooting its veins all round the obred heaven
Red rose the clouds from the Atlantic in vast wheels of blood,
And in the red clouds rose a Wonder o'er the Atlantic sea
Intense! naked! a Human fire, fierce glowing as the wedge
Of iron heated in the furnace; his terrible limbs were fire,
With myriads of cloudy terrors, banners dark, & towers
Surrounded; heat but not light went thro' the murky atmosphere.
The King of England looking westward trembles at the vision.

PLATE 5

Albion's Angel stood beside the Stone of night, and saw
The terror like a comet, or more like the planet red
That once enclos'd the terrible wandering comets in its sphere.
Then, Mars, thou wast our centre, & the planets three flew round
Thy crimson disk; so, e'er the Sun was rent from thy red sphere,
The Spectre glow'd, his horrid length staining the temple long
With beams of blood; & thus a voice came forth, and shook the temple:

PLATE 6

'The morning comes, the night decays, the watchmen leave their stations;
The grave is burst, the spices shed, the linen wrapped up;
The bones of death, the cov'ring clay, the sinews shrunk & dry'd
Reviving shake, inspiring move, breathing! awakening!
Spring like redeemed captives when their bonds & bars are burst.
Let the slave grinding at the mill run out into the field,
Let him look up into the heavens & laugh in the bright air;
Let the inchained soul, shut up in darkness and in sighing,
Whose face has never seen a smile in thirty weary years,
Rise and look out; his chains are loose, his dungeon doors are open.
And let his wife and children return from the oppressor's scourge;
They look behind at every step & believe it is a dream,
Singing: "The Sun has left his blackness, & has found a fresher morning,
And the fair Moon rejoices in the clear & cloudless night;
For Empire is no more, and now the Lion & Wolf shall cease."

PLATE 7

In thunders ends the voice. Then Albion's Angel wrathful burnt

Beside the Stone of Night and like the Eternal Lion's howl
In famine & war reply'd: 'Art thou not Orc, who serpent-form'd
Stands at the gate of Enitharmon to devour her children?
Blasphemous Demon, Antichrist, hater of Dignities,
Lover of wild rebellion, and transgressor of God's Law,
Why dost thou come to Angel's eyes in this terrific form?'

PLATE 8

The terror answe'd: 'I am Orc, wreath'd round the accursed tree
The times are ended; shadows pass, the morning' gins to break;
The fiery joy that Urizen perverted to ten commands,
What night he led the starry hosts thro' the wide wilderness,
That stony law I stamp to dust, and scatter religion abroad
To the four winds as a torn book, & none shall gather the leaves;
But they shall rot on desert sands, & consume in bottomless deeps,
To make the desarts blossom & the deeps shrink to their fountains,
And to renew the fiery joy, and burst the stony roof;
That pale religious lechery, seeking Virginity,
May find it in a harlot, and in coarse-clad honesty
The undefil'd, tho' ravish'd in her cradle night and morn;
For every thing that lives is holy, life delights in life;
Because the soul of sweet delight can never be defil'd.
Fires enwrap the earthly globe, yet Man is not consum'd;
Amidst the lustful fires he walks; his feet become like brass,
His knees and thighs like silver, & his breast and head like gold'.

PLATE 9

'Sound! sound! my loud war-trumpets & alarm my Thirteen Angels!
Loud howls the eternal Wolf! the eternal Lion lashes his tail!
America is dark'ned, and my punishing Demons terrified,
Crouch howling before their caverns deep like skins dry'd in the wind.

They cannot smite the wheat, nor quench the fatness of the earth;
They cannot smite with sorrows, nor subdue the plough and spade;
They cannot wall the city, nor moat round the castle of princes;
They cannot bring the stubbed oak to overgrow the hills.
For terrible men stand on the shores, & in their robes I see
Children take shelter from the lightnings; there stands Washington
And Paine and Warren with their foreheads rear'd toward the east.
But clouds obscure my aged sight. A vision from afar!
Sound! sound! my loud war-trumpets & alarm my thirteen Angels.
Ah, vision from afar! Ah, rebel form that rent the ancient
Heavens! Eternal Viper self-renew'd, rolling in clouds,
I see thee in thick clouds and darkness on America's shore,
Writhing in pangs of abhorred birth. Red flames the crest rebellious
And eyes of death. The harlot womb, oft opened in vain,
Heaves in enormous circles; now the times are return'd upon thee,
Devourer of thy parent; now thy unutterable torment renews.
Sound! sound! my loud war trumpets & alarm my thirteen Angels.
Ah, terrible birth! a young one bursting! where is the weeping mouth?
And where the mother's milk? Instead, those ever-hissing jaws
And parched lips drop with fresh gore. Now roll thou in the clouds.
Thy mother lays her length outstretch'd upon the shore beneath.
Sound! sound! my loud war-trumpets & alarm my Thirteen Angels!
Loud howls the eternal Wolf; the eternal Lion lashes his tail!'

PLATE 10

Thus wept the Angel voice, & as he wept the terrible blasts
Of trumpets blew a loud alarm across the Atlantic deep.

No trumpets answer; no reply of clarions or of fifes;
Silent the Colonies remain and refuse the loud alarm.
On those vast shady hills between America & Albion's shore,
Now barr'd out by the Atlantic sea, call'd Atlantean hills
Because from their bright summits you may pass to the Golden world,
An ancient palace, archetype of mighty Emperies,
Rears its immortal pinnacles, built in the forest of God
By Ariston the king of beauty, for his stolen bride.
Here on their magic seats the thirteen Angels sat perturb'd,
For clouds from the Atlantic hover o'er the solemn roof.

PLATE 11

Fiery the Angels rose, & as they rose deep thunder roll'd
Around their shores, indignant burning with the fires of Orc;
And Boston's Angel cried aloud as they flew thro' the dark night.
He cried: 'Why trembles honesty, and like a murderer,
Why seeks he refuge from the frowns of his immortal station?
Must the generous tremble, & leave his joy to the idle, to the pestilence,
That mock him? Who commanded this? what God? what Angel?
To keep the gen'rous from experience till the ungenerous
Are unrestrain'd performers of the energies of nature;
Till pity is become a trade, and generosity a science
That men get rich by, & the sandy desart is giv'n to the strong.
What God is he writes laws of peace, and clothes him in a tempest?
What pitying Angel lusts for tears, & fans himself with sighs?
What crawling villain preaches abstinence & wraps himself
In fat of lambs? No more I follow, no more obedience pay!'

PLATE 12

So cried he, rending off his robe & throwing down his scepter
In sight of Albion's Guardian; and all the thirteen Angels
Rent off their robes to the hungry wind, & threw their golden scepters
Down on the land of America. Indignant they descended

Headlong from out their heavenly heights, descending swift as fires
Over the land; naked & flaming are their lineaments seen
In the deep gloom. By Washington & Paine & Warren they stood;
And the flame folded, roaring fierce within the pitchy night
Before the Demon red, who burnt towards America
In black smoke, thunders, and loud winds, rejoicing in its terror,
Breaking in smoky wreaths from the wild deep, & gath'ring thick
In flames as of a furnace on the land from North to South.

PLATE 13

What time the thirteen Governors, that England sent convene
In Bernard's house, the flames cover'd the land. They rouse; they cry;
Shaking their mental chains they rush in fury to the sea
To quench their anguish; at the feet of Washington down fall'n
They grovel on the sand and writhing lie, while all
The British soldiers thro' the thirteen states sent up a howl
Of anguish, threw their swords & muskets to the earth & ran
From their encampments and dark castles, seeking where to hide
From the grim flames and from the visions of Orc; in sight
Of Albion's Angel, who, enrag'd his secret clouds open'd
From north to south, and burnt outstretch'd on wings of wrath, cov'ring
The eastern sky, spreading his awful wings across the heavens.
Beneath him roll'd his num'rous hosts; all Albion's Angels camp'd
Darken'd the Atlantic mountains, & their trumpets shook the valleys,
Arm'd with diseases of the earth to cast upon the Abyss,
Their numbers forty millions, must'ring in the eastern sky.

PLATE 14

In the flames stood & view'd the armies drawn out in the sky,
Washington, Franklin, Paine, & Warren, Allen, Gates, & Lee,

And heard the voice of Albion's Angel give the thunderous command.
His plagues, obedient to his voice, flew forth out of their clouds,
Falling upon America, as a storm to cut them off
As a blight cuts the tender corn when it begins to appear.
Dark is the heaven above, & cold & hard the earth beneath;
And as a plague wind fill'd with insects cuts off man & beast,
And, as a sea o'erwhelms a land in the day of an earthquake,
Fury rage madness! in a wind swept through America;
And the red flames of Orc that folded roaring fierce around
The angry shores, and the fierce rushing of th' inhabitants together.
The citizens of New-York close their books & lock their chests;
The mariners of Boston drop their anchors and unlade;
The scribe of Pensylvania casts his pen upon the earth;
The builder of Virginia throws his hammer down in fear.
Then had America been lost, o'erwhelm'd by the Atlantic,
And Earth had lost another portion of the infinite;
But all rush together in the night in wrath and raging fire.
The red fires rag'd! the plagues recoil'd! then roll'd they back with fury

PLATE 15

On Albion's Angels. Then the Pestilence began in streaks of red
Across the limbs of Albion's Guardian; the spotted plague smote Bristol's,
And the Leprosy London's Spirit, sickening all their bands.
The millions sent up a howl of anguish and threw off their hammer'd mail,
And cast their swords & spears to earth, & stood a naked multitude.
Albion's Guardian writhed in torment on the eastern sky,
Pale, quiv'ring toward the brain his glimmering eyes, teeth chattering,
Howling & shuddering, his legs quivering, convuls'd each muscle & sinew.
Sick'ning lay London's Guardian, and the ancient miter'd York,

Their heads on snowy hills, their ensigns sick'ning in the sky.
The plagues creep on the burning winds, driven by flames of Orc,
And by the fierce Americans rushing together in the night,
Driven o'er the Guardians of Ireland and Scotland and Wales.
They, spotted with plagues, forsook the frontiers, & their banners sear'd
With fires of hell deform their ancient heavens with shame & woe.
Hid in his caves the Bard of Albion felt the enormous plagues,
And a cowl of flesh grew o'er his head, & scales on his back & ribs;
And, rough with black scales, all his Angels fright their ancient heavens.
The doors of marriage are open, and the Priests in rustling scales
Rush into reptile coverts, hiding from the fires of Orc
That play around the golden roofs in wreaths of fierce desire,
Leaving the females naked and glowing with the lusts of youth.
For the female spirits of the dead, pining in bonds of religion,
Run from their fetters reddening, & in long drawn arches sitting
They feel the nerves of youth renew, and desires of ancient times
Over their pale limbs as a vine when the tender grape appears.

PLATE 16

Over the hills, the vales, the cities, rage the red flames fierce;
The Heavens melted from north to south; and Urizen, who sat
Above all heavens in thunders wrap'd, emerg'd his leprous head
From out his holy shrine, his tears in deluge piteous
Falling into the deep sublime; Flag'd with grey-brow'd snows
And thunderous visages, his jealous wings wav'd over the deep;
Weeping in dismal howling woe he dark descended, howling
Around the smitten bands, clothed in tears & trembling shudd'ring cold.

His stored snows he poured forth, and his icy magazine
He open'd on the deep and on the Atlantic sea white shiv'ring
Leprous his limbs, all over white, and hoary was his visage,
Weeping in dismal howlings before the stern Americans,
Hiding the Demon red with clouds & cold mists from the earth;
Till Angels & weak men twelve years should govern o'er the strong,
And then their end should come, when France receiv'd the Demon's light
Stiff shudderings shook the heav'nly thrones! France, Spain, and Italy
In terror view'd the bands of Albion, and the ancient Guardians,
Fainting upon the elements, smitten with their own plagues!
They slow advance to shut the five gates of their law-built heaven,
Filled with blasting fancies and with mildews of despair,
With fierce disease and lust, unable to stem the fires of Orc.
But the five gates were consum'd, & their bolts and hinges melted.
And the fierce flames burnt round the heavens, & round the abodes of men.

EUROPE

A Prophecy

PLATE 3

'Five windows light the cavern'd Man: thro' one he breathes the air;
Thro' one hears music of the spheres; thro' one the eternal Vine
Flourishes, that he may receive the grapes; thro' one can look
And see small portions of the eternal world that ever groweth;
Thro' one himself pass out what time he please, but he will not;
For stolen joys are sweet, & bread eaten in secret pleasant.'
So sang a Fairy mocking as he sat on a streak'd Tulip,
Thinking none saw him; when he ceas'd I started from the trees,

And caught him in my hat, as boys knock down a butterfly.
'How know you this,' said I, 'small Sir? where did you learn this song?
Seeing himself in my possession, thus he answer'd me:
'My Master, I am yours; command me, for I must obey.'
'Then tell me what is the material world and is it dead?'
He, laughing, answer'd: 'I will write a book on leaves of flowers,
If you will feed me on love-thoughts, & give me now and then
A cup of sparkling poetic fancies. So, when I am tipsie,
I'll sing to you to this soft lute, and shew you all alive
The world, where every particle of dust breathes forth its joy.'
I took him home in my warm bosom. As we went along
Wild flowers I gather'd & he shew'd me each eternal flower.
He laugh'd aloud to see them whimper because they were pluck'd.
They hover'd round me like a cloud of incense. When I came
Into my parlour and sat down, and took my pen to write,
My Fairy sat upon the table, and dictated 'EUROPE.'

Preludium

PLATE 1

The nameless shadowy female rose from out the breast of Orc,
Her snaky hair brandishing in the winds of Enitharmon;
And thus her voice arose:
'O mother Enitharmon, wilt thou bring forth other sons,
To cause my name to vanish, that my place may not be found?
For I am faint with travel!
Like the dark cloud disburden'd in the day of dismal thunder.
My roots are brandish'd in the heavens, my fruits in earth beneath
Surge, foam, and labour into life, first born & first consum'd!
Consumed and consuming!
Then why shouldst thou, Accursed mother, bring me into life?
'I wrap my turban of thick clouds around my lab'ring head,
And fold the sheety waters as a mantle round my limbs.
Yet the red sun and moon
And all the overflowing stars rain down prolific pains.

PLATE 2

'Unwilling I look up to heaven! unwilling count the stars!
Sitting in fathomless abyss of my immortal shrine,
I seize their burning power
And bring forth howling terrors, all devouring fiery kings,
'Devouring & devoured, roaming on dark and desolate mountains
In forests of eternal death, shrieking in hollow trees.
Ah mother Enitharmon!
Stamp not with solid form this vig'rous progeny of fires.
'I bring forth from my teeming bosom myriads of flames,
And thou dost stamp them with a signet; then they roam abroad
And leave me void as death.
Ah! I am drown'd in shady woe, and visionary joy.
'And who shall bind the infinite with an eternal band?
To compass it with swaddling bands? and who shall cherish it
With milk and honey?
I see it smile & I roll inward, & my voice is past.'
She ceas'd & roll'd her shady clouds
Into the secret place.

A Prophecy

PLATE 3

The deep of winter came,
What time the secret child
Descended through the orient gates of the Eternal day.
War ceas'd & all the troops like shadows fled to their abodes.
Then Enitharmon saw her sons & daughters rise around;
Like pearly clouds they meet together in the crystal house;
And Los, possessor of the moon, joy'd in the peaceful night,
Thus speaking, while his num'rous sons shook their bright fiery wings:

'Again the night is come
That strong Urthona takes his rest,
And Urizen, unloos'd from chains,
Glows like a meteor in the distant north.
Stretch forth your hands and strike the elemental strings!
Awake the thunders of the deep,

PLATE 4

'The shrill winds wake!
Till all the sons of Urizen look out and envy Los:
Seize all the spirits of life and bind
Their warbling joys to our loud strings;
Bind all the nourishing sweets of earth
To give us bliss, that we may drink the sparkling wine of Los;
And let us laugh at war,
Despising toil and care,
Because the days and nights of joy in lucky hours renew.'

'Arise, O Orc, from thy deep den,
First born of Enitharmon, rise!
And we will crown thy head with garlands of the ruddy vine;
For now thou art bound,
And I may see thee in the hour of bliss, my eldest born.'

The horrent Demon rose, surrounded with red stars of fire,
Whirling about in furious circles round the immortal fiend.

Then Enitharmon down descended into his red light,
And thus her voice rose to her children; the distant heavens reply:

PLATE 5

'Now comes the night of Enitharmon's joy!
Who shall I call? Who shall I send?
That Woman, lovely Woman! may have dominion?
Arise, O Rintrah, thee I call! & Palamabron, thee!
Go! tell the human race that Woman's love is Sin;
That an eternal life awaits the worms of sixty winters
In an allegorical abode, where existence hath never come.
Forbid all Joy, & from her childhood shall the little female
Spread nets in every secret path.

'My weary eyelids draw towards the evening, my bliss is yet but new!

PLATE 8

'Arise, O Rintrah, eldest born, second to none but Orc.
O lion Rintrah, raise thy fury from thy forests black;
Bring Palamabron, horned priest, skipping upon the mountains,
And silent Elynittria, the silver bowed queen.
Rintrah, where hast thou hid thy bride?
Weeps she in desart shades?
Alas! my Rintrah! bring the lovely jealous Ocalythron.

'Arise, my son! bring all thy brethren, O thou king of fire.
Prince of the sun, I see thee with thy innumerable race,
Thick as the summer stars;
But each ramping his golden mane shakes,
And thine eyes rejoice because of strength, O Rintrah, furious king.'

PLATE 9

Enitharmon slept,
Eighteen hundred years. Man was a Dream!
The night of Nature and their harps unstrung.
She slept in middle of her nightly song,
Eighteen hundred years, a female dream.
Shadows of men in fleeting bands upon the winds
Divide the heavens of Europe,
Till Albion's Angel, smitten with his own plagues, fled with his bands.
The cloud bears hard on Albion's shore,
Fill'd with immortal demons of futurity.
In council gather the smitten Angels of Albion.
The cloud bears hard upon the council house, down rushing
On the heads of Albion's Angels.

One hour they lay buried beneath the ruins of that hall;
But as the stars rise from the salt lake they arise in pain,
In troubled mists o'erclouded by the terrors of strugling times.

PLATE 10

In thoughts perturb'd they rose from the bright ruins, silent following
The fiery King, who sought his ancient temple serpent-form'd,
That stretches out its shady length along the Island white.
Round him roll'd his clouds of war; silent the Angel went,
Along the infinite shores of Thames to golden Verulam.
There stand the venerable porches that high-towering rear
Their oak-surrounded pillars, form'd of massy stones, uncut
With tool, stones precious!—such eternal in the heavens,
Of colours twelve, few known on earth, give light in the opake,
Plac'd in the order of the stars. When the five senses whelm'd
In deluge o'er the earth-born man, then turn'd the fluxile eyes
Into two stationary orbs, concentrating all things;
The ever-varying spiral ascents to the heavens of heavens
Were bended downward, and the nostrils' golden gate shut,
Turn'd outward, barr'd and petrify'd against the Infinite.

Thought chang'd the infinite to a serpent, that which pitieth
To a devouring flame; and man fled from its face and hid
In forests of night. Then all the eternal forests were divided
Into earths rolling in circles of space, that like an ocean rush'd
And overwhelmed all except this finite wall of flesh.
Then was the serpent temple form'd, image of infinite
Shut up in finite revolutions, and man became an Angel,
Heaven a mighty circle turning, God a tyrant crown'd

Now arriv'd the ancient Guardian at the southern porch
That, planted thick with trees of blackest leaf, & in a vale
Obscure enclos'd the stone of Night. Oblique it stood, o'erhung
With purple flowers and berries red, image of that sweet south
Once open to the heavens and elevated on the human neck,
Now overgrown with hair and cover'd with a stony roof.
Downward 'tis sunk beneath th' attractive north, that round the feet
A raging whirlpool draws the dizzy enquirer to his grave.

PLATE 11

Albion's Angel rose upon the Stone of Night.
He saw Urizen on the Atlantic;
And his brazen Book
That Kings & Priests had copied on earth.
Expanded from North to South.

PLATE 12

And the clouds & fires pale roll'd round in the night of Enitharmon,
Round Albion's cliffs & London's walls (still Enitharmon slept);
Rolling volumes of grey mist involve Churches, Palaces, Towers;
For Urizen unclasp'd his Book, feeding his soul with pity.
The youth of England, hid in gloom, curse the pain'd heavens, compell'd
Into the deadly night to see the form of Albion's Angel.
Their parents brought them forth, & Aged Ignorance preaches, canting,
On a vast rock, perceived by those senses that are clos'd from thought—
Bleak, dark, abrupt it stands, & overshadows London city.
They saw his boney feet on the rock, the flesh consum'd in flames;
They saw the Serpent temple lifted above, shadowing the Island white;
They heard the voice of Albion's Angel howling in flames of Orc,
Seeking the trump of the last doom.
Above the rest the howl was heard from Westminster, louder and louder.
The Guardian of the secret codes forsook his ancient mansion,
Driven out by the flames of Orc; his furr'd robes & false locks
Adhered and grew one with his flesh, and nerves, & veins shot thro' them.
With dismal torment sick, hanging upon the wind, he fled
Groveling, along Great George Street thro' the Park gate; all the soldiers
Fled from his sight; he drag'd his torments to the wilderness.
Thus was the howl thro' Europe!

For Orc rejoic'd to hear the howling shadows;
But Palamabron shot his lightnings trenching down his wide back,
And Rintrah hung with all his legions in the nether deep.
Enitharmon laugh'd in her sleep to see (O woman's triumph)
Every house a den, every man bound; the shadows are fill'd
With spectres, and the windows wove over with curses of iron;
Over the doors 'Thou shalt not', & over the chimneys 'Fear' is written;
With bands of iron round their necks fasten'd into the walls
The citizens; in leaden gyves the inhabitants of suburbs
Walk heavy; soft and bent are the bones of villagers.
Between the clouds of Urizen the flames of Orc roll heavy
Around the limbs of Albion's Guardian, his flesh consuming.
Howlings & hissings, shrieks & groans, & voices of despair
Arise around him in the cloudy Heavens of Albion. Furious,

PLATE 13

The red limb'd Angel seiz'd in horror and torment,
The Trump of the last doom; but he could not blow the iron tube!
Thrice he assay'd presumptuous to awake the dead to Judgment.
A mighty Spirit leap'd from the land of Albion,
Nam'd Newton; he seiz'd the Trump & blow'd the enormous blast!
Yellow as leaves of Autumn the myriads of Angelic hosts
Fell thro' the wintry skies seeking their graves,
Rattling their hollow bones in howling and lamentation.
Then Enitharmon woke, nor knew that she had slept;
And eighteen hundred years were fled
As if they had not been.
She call'd her sons & daughters
To the sports of night,
Within her crystal house;
And thus her song proceeds:

'Arise, Ethinthus! tho' the earth-worm call,
Let him call in vain;

Till the night of holy shadows
And human solitude is past!

PLATE 14

'Ethinthus, queen of waters, how thou shinest in the sky!
My daughter, how do I rejoice! for thy children flock around
Like the gay fishes on the wave when the cold moon drinks the dew.
Ethinthus! thou art sweet as comforts to my fainting soul,
For now thy waters warble round the feet of Enitharmon.
'Manathu-Varcyon! I behold thee flaming in my halls,
Light of thy mother's soul! I see thy lovely eagles round;
Thy golden wings are my delight, & thy flames of soft delusion.

'where is my luring bird of Eden? Leutha, silent love!
Leutha, the many colour'd bow delights upon thy wings,
Soft soul of flowers, Leutha!
Sweet smiling pestilence! I see thy blushing light;
Thy daughters many changing
Revolve like sweet perfumes ascending, O Leutha, silken queen!
'Where is the youthful Antamon, prince of the pearly dew?
O Antamon, why wilt thou leave thy mother Enitharmon?
Alone I see thee, crystal form,
Floating upon the bosom'd air
With lineaments of gratified desire.
My Antamon, the seven churches of Leutha seek thy love.

'I hear the soft Oothoon in Enitharmon's tents.
Why wilt thou give up woman's secrecy my melancholy child?
Between two moments bliss is ripe
O Theotormon robb'd of joy, I see thy salt tears flow
Down the steps of my crystal house.
'Sotha & Thiralatha, secret dwellers of dreamful caves,
Arise and please the horrent fiend with your melodious songs.
Still all your thunders golden hoof'd, & bind horses black.
Orc! smile upon my children!
Smile, son of my afflictions.
Arise, O Orc, and give our mountains joy of thy red light.'

She ceas'd; for all were forth at sport beneath the solemn moon,
Waking the stars of Urizen with their immortal songs,
That nature felt thro' all her pores the enormous revelry,
Till morning oped the eastern gate.
Then every one fled to his station, & Enitharmon wept.
But terrible Orc, when he beheld the morning in the east,

PLATE 15

Shot from the heights of Enitharmon,
And in the vineyard of red France appear'd the light of his fury.
The sun glow'd fiery red!
The furious terrors tlew around
On golden chariots raging, with red wheels dropping with blood;
The Lions lash their wrathful tails,
The Tigers couch upon the prey & suck the ruddy tide;
And Enitharmon groans & cries in anguish and dismay.
Then Los arose; his head he rear'd in snaky thunders clad,
And with a cry that shook all nature to the utmost pole
Call'd all his sons to the strife of blood.

FIRST BOOK OF URIZEN

Preludium

PLATE 2

Of the primeval Priest's assum'd power,
When Eternals spurn'd back his religion,
And gave him a place in the north,
Obscure, shadowy, void, solitary.

Eternals, I hear your call gladly.
Dictate swift winged words, & fear not
To unfold your dark visions of torment.

PLATE 3

CHAP. I

1. Lo, a shadow of horror is risen
In Eternity! Unknown, unprolific,
Self-clos'd, all-repelling: what Demon
Hath form'd this abominable void,
This soul-shudd'ring vacuum? Some said,
'It is Urizen.' But unknown, abstracted,
Brooding, secret, the dark power hid.

2. Times on times he divided, & measur'd
Space by space in his ninefold darkness,
Unseen, unknown; changes appear'd
In his desolate mountains, rifted furious
By the black winds of perturbation.

3. For he strove in battles dire,
In unseen conflictions with shapes
Bred from his forsaken wilderness,
Of beast, bird, fish, serpent, & element,
Combustion, blast, vapour and cloud.

4. Dark revolving in silent activity,
Unseen in tormenting passions,
An activity unknown and horrible,
A self-contemplating shadow,
In enormous labours occupied.

5. But Eternals beheld his vast forests.
Age on ages he lay, clos'd, unknown,
Brooding, shut in the deep; all avoid
The petrific abominable chaos.

6. His cold horrors silent, dark Urizen
Prepar'd; his ten thousands of thunders
Rang'd in gloom'd array stretch out across
The dread world; & the rolling of wheels,
As of swelling seas, sound in his clouds,
In his hills of stor'd snows, in his mountains
Of hail & ice; voices of terror
Are heard, like thunders of autumn,
When the cloud blazes over the harvests.

CHAP. II

1. Earth was not, nor globes of attraction.
The will of the Immortal expanded
Or contracted his all flexible senses.
Death was not, but eternal life sprung.

2. The sound of a trumpet the heavens
Awoke, & vast clouds of blood roll'd
Round the dim rocks of Urizen, so nam'd,
That solitary one in Immensity.

3. Shrill the trumpet; & myriads of Eternity

PLATE 4

Muster around the bleak desarts,
Now fill'd with clouds, darkness, & waters
That roll'd perplex'd lab'ring, & utter'd
Words articulate, bursting in thunders,
That roll'd on the tops of his mountains:

4. 'From the depths of dark solitude; from
The eternal abode in my holiness,
Hidden, set apart in my stern counsels
Reserv'd for the days of futurity,
I have sought for a joy without pain,
For a solid without fluctuation.
Why will you die, O Eternals?
Why live in unquenchable burnings?

5. 'First I fought with the fire, consum'd
Inwards into a deep world within—
A void immense, wild, dark & deep,
Where nothing was, Nature's wide womb.
And self-balanc'd, stretch'd o'er the void,
I alone, even I! the winds merciless
Bound; but condensing, in torrents
They fall and fall; strong I repell'd
The vast waves, & arose on the waters
A wide world of solid obstruction.

6. 'Here alone I, in books form'd of metals,
Have written the secrets of wisdom,
The secrets of dark contemplation,

By fightings and conflicts dire
With terrible monsters Sin-bred,
Which the bosoms of all inhabit,
Seven deadly Sins of the soul.

7. 'Lo! I unfold my darkness, and on
This rock place with strong hand the Book
Of eternal brass, written in my solitude:

8. 'Laws of peace, of love, of unity,
Of pity, compassion, forgiveness.
Let each chuse one habitation,
His ancient infinite mansion,
One command, one joy, one desire,
One curse, one weight, one measure,
One King, one God, one Law.'

CHAP. III

1. The voice ended. They saw his pale visage
Emerge from the darkness, his hand
On the rock of eternity unclasping
The Book of brass. Rage seiz'd the strong

2. Rage, fury, intense indignation,
In cataracts of fire, blood, & gall,
In whirlwinds of sulphurous smoke
And enormous forms of energy;
All the seven deadly sins of the soul

PLATE 5

In living creations appear'd
In the flames of eternal fury.

3. Sund'ring, dark'ning, thund'ring!
Rent away with a terrible crash,
Eternity roll'd wide apart,
Wide asunder rolling

Mountainous, all around
Departing, departing, departing,
Leaving ruinous fragments of life,
Hanging, frowning cliffs, & all between
An ocean of voidness unfathomable.

4. The roaring fires ran o'er the heav'ns
In whirlwinds & cataracts of blood,
And o'er the dark desarts of Urizen
Fires pour thro' the void on all sides
On Urizen's self-begotten armies.

5. But no light from the fires: all was darkness
In the flames of Eternal fury.

6. In fierce anguish & quenchless flames
To the desarts and rocks he ran raging
To hide, but he could not; combining,
He dug mountains & hills in vast strength;
He piled them in incessant labour,
In howlings & pangs & fierce madness,
Long periods in burning fires labouring,
Till hoary, and age-broke, and aged,
In despair and the shadows of death.

7. And a roof vast, petrific, around,
On all sides he fram'd; like a womb,
Where thousands of rivers in veins
Of blood pour down the mountains to cool
The eternal fires beating without
From Eternals; & like a black globe.
View'd by sons of Eternity, standing
On the shore of the infinite ocean,
Like a human heart strugling & beating,
The vast world of Urizen appear'd.

8. And Los round the dark globe of Urizen
Kept watch for Eternals to confine
The obscure separation alone;
For Eternity stood wide apart,

PLATE 6

As the stars are apart from the earth.

9. Los wept howling around the dark Demon,
And cursing his lot; for in anguish
Urizen was rent from his side,
And a fathomless void for his feet,

And intense fires for his dwelling.

10. But Urizen laid in a stony sleep,
Unorganiz'd, rent from Eternity.

11. The Eternals said: 'What is this? Death.
Urizen is a clod of clay.'

PLATE 7

12. Los howl'd in a dismal stupor,
Groaning! gnashing! groaning!
Till the wrenching apart was heared.

13. But the wrenching of Urizen heal'd not.
Cold, featureless, flesh or clay,
Rifted with direful changes,
He lay in a dreamless night,

14. Till Los rouz'd his fires, affrighted
At the formless unmeasurable death.

PLATE 8 CHAP. IV[A]

1. Los, smitten with astonishment,
Frighten'd at the hurtling bones

2. And at the surging sulphureous
Perturbed Immortal, mad raging

3. In whirlwinds & pitch & nitre
Round the furious limbs of Los.

4. And Los formed nets & gins
And threw the nets round about.

5. He watch'd in shudd'ring fear
The dark changes, & bound every change
With rivets of iron & brass.

6. And these were the changes of Urizen:

PLATE 10 CHAP. IV[B]

1. Ages on ages roll'd over him!
In stony sleep ages roll'd over him!
Like a dark waste stretching, chang'able,
By earthquakes riv'n, belching sullen fires.

On ages roll'd ages in ghastly
Sick torment; around him in whirlwinds
Of darkness the eternal Prophet howl'd,
Beating still on his rivets of iron,
Pouring sodor of iron, dividing
The horrible night into watches.

2. And Urizen (so his eternal name)
His prolific delight obscur'd more & more
In dark secrecy, hiding in surgeing
Sulphureous fluid his phantasies.
The Eternal Prophet heav'd the dark bellows,
And turn'd restless the tongs, & the hammer
Incessant beat, forging chains new & new,
Numb'ring with links hours, days & years.

3. The Eternal mind, bounded, began to roll
Eddies of wrath ceaseless round & round,
And the sulphureous foam surgeing thick
Settled, a lake, bright & shining clear,
White as the snow on the mountains cold.

4. Forgetfulness, dumbness, necessity!
In chains of the mind locked up,
Like fetters of ice shrinking together,
Disorganiz'd, rent from Eternity.
Los beat on his fetters of iron,
And heated his furnaces, and pour'd
Iron sodor and sodor of brass.

5. Restless turn'd the immortal, inchain'd,
Heaving dolorous, anguish'd, unbearable,
Till a roof, shaggy, wild, inclos'd
In an orb his fountain of thought.

6. In a horrible dreamful slumber,
Like the linked infernal chain,
A vast Spine writh'd in torment
Upon the winds, shooting pain'd
Ribs, like a bending cavern;
And bones of solidness froze
Over all his nerves of joy.

And a first Age passed over,
And a state of dismal woe.

PLATE 11

7. From the caverns of his jointed Spine
Down sunk with fright a red
Round globe, hot burning, deep
Deep down into the Abyss,
Panting, Conglobing, Trembling,
Shooting out ten thousand branches
Around his solid bones
And a second Age passed over,
And a state of dismal woe.

8. In harrowing fear rolling round,
His nervous brain shot branches
Round the branches of his heart
On high into two little orbs;
And fixed in two little caves
Hiding carefully from the wind,
His Eyes beheld the deep.
And a third Age passed over,
And a state of dismal woe.

9. The pangs of hope began
In heavy pain, striving, struggling.
Two Ears, in close volutions
From beneath his orbs of vision
Shot spiring out and petrified
As they grew. And a fourth Age passed,
And a state of dismal woe.

10. In ghastly torment sick,
Hanging upon the wind,

PLATE 13

Two Nostrils bent down to the deep.
And a fifth Age passed over,
And a state of dismal woe.

11. In ghastly torment sick,
Within his ribs bloated round,
A craving, Hungry Cavern.
Thence arose his channel'd Throat,
And like a red flame a Tongue
Of thirst & of hunger appear'd.
And a sixth Age passed over,
And a state of dismal woe.

12. Enraged & stifled with torment,
He threw his right Arm to the north,
His left Arm to the south
Shooting out in anguish deep;
And his Feet stamp'd the nether Abyss
In trembling & howling and dismay.
And a seventh Age passed over,
And a state of dismal woe.

CHAP. V

1. In terrors Los shrunk from his task.
His great hammer fell from his hand;
His fires beheld, and sickening
Hid their strong limbs in smoke.
For with noises, ruinous loud,
With hurtlings & clashings & groans,
The Immortal endur'd his chains,
Tho' bound in a deadly sleep.

2. All the myriads of Eternity,
All the wisdom & joy of life,
Roll like a sea around him,
Except what his little orbs
Of sight by degrees unfold.

3. And now his eternal life,
Like a dream was obliterated.

4. Shudd'ring, the Eternal Prophet smote
With a stroke from his north to south region.
The bellows & hammer are silent now.
A nerveless silence his prophetic voice
Seiz'd; a cold solitude & dark void
The Eternal Prophet & Urizen clos'd.

5. Ages on ages roll'd over them,
Cut off from life & light, frozen
Into horrible forms of deformity.
Los suffer'd his fires to decay;
Then he look'd back with anxious desire,
But the space, undivided by existence,
Struck horror into his soul.

6. Los wept, obscur'd with mourning;
His bosom earthquak'd with sighs;
He saw Urizen deadly black,
In his chains bound, & Pity began,

7. In anguish dividing & dividing
(For pity divides the soul)
In pangs, eternity on eternity.
Life in cataracts pour'd down his cliffs.
The void shrunk the lymph into Nerves,
Wand'ring wide on the bosom of night,
And left a round globe of blood
Trembling upon the void.

PLATE 15

Thus the Eternal Prophet was divided
Before the death image of Urizen;
For in changeable clouds and darkness,
In a winterly night beneath,
The Abyss of Los stretch'd immense;
And now seen, now obscur'd to the eyes
Of Eternals, the visions remote
Of the dark separation appear'd.
As glasses discover Worlds
In the endless Abyss of space,
So the expanding eyes of Immortals
Beheld the dark visions of Los,
And the globe of life blood trembling.

PLATE 18

8. The globe of life blood trembled,
Branching out into roots,
Fibrous, writhing upon the winds,
Fibres of blood, milk and tears,
In pangs eternity on eternity.
At length, in tears & cries embodied,
A female form, trembling and pale,
Waves before his deathy face.

9. All Eternity shudder'd at sight
Of the first female now separate,
Pale as a cloud of snow,
Waving before the face of Los.

10. Wonder, awe, fear, astonishment
Petrify the eternal myriads
At the first female form now separate.

PLATE 19

They call'd her Pity, and fled:

11. 'Spread a Tent with strong curtains around them;
Let cords & stakes bind in the Void,
That Eternals may no more behold them.'

12. They began to weave curtains of darkness;
They erected large pillars round the Void,
With golden hooks fasten'd in the pillars;
With infinite labour the Eternals
A woof wove, and called it Science.

CHAP. VI

1. But Los saw the Female & pitied.
He embrac'd her; she wept, she refus'd.
In perverse and cruel delight;
She fled from his arms, yet he follow'd.

2. Eternity shudder'd when they saw
Man begetting his likeness
On his own divided Image.

3. A time passed over; the Eternals
Began to erect the tent;
When Enitharmon, sick,
Felt a Worm within her womb.

4. Yet helpless it lay like a Worm
In the trembling womb,
To be moulded into existence.

5. All day the worm lay on her bosom;
All night within her womb
The worm lay, till it grew to a serpent,
With dolorous hissings & poisons
Round Enitharmon's loins folding.

6. Coil'd within Enitharmon's womb
The serpent grew, casting its scales;
With sharp pangs the hissings began
To change to a grating cry.
Many sorrows and dismal throes,
Many forms of fish, bird, & beast,
Brought forth an Infant form
Where was a worm before.

7. The Eternals their tent finished,
Alarm'd with these gloomy visions,
When Enitharmon groaning
Produc'd a man Child to the light.

8. A shriek ran thro' Eternity,
And a paralytic stroke,
At the birth of the Human shadow.

9. Delving earth in his resistless way,
Howling, the Child with fierce flames
Issu'd from Enitharmon.

10. The Eternals closed the tent;
They beat down the stakes; the cords

PLATE 20

Stretch'd for a work of eternity;
No more Los beheld Eternity.

11. In his hands he seiz'd the Infant;
He bathed him in springs of sorrow;
He gave him to Enitharmon.

CHAP. VII

1. They named the child Orc; he grew,
Fed with milk of Enitharmon.

2. Los awoke her. O sorrow & pain!
A tight'ning girdle grew
Around his bosom. In sobbings
He burst the girdle in twain,
But still another girdle
Oppress'd his bosom. In sobbings
Again he burst it. Again
Another girdle succeeds.
The girdle was form'd by day,
By night was burst in twain.

3. These falling down on the rock
Into an iron Chain
In each other link by link lock'd.

4. They took Orc to the top of a mountain.
O how Enitharmon wept!
They chain'd his young limbs to the rock
With the Chain of Jealousy
Beneath Urizen's deathful shadow.

5. The dead heard the voice of the child,
And began to awake from sleep.
All things heard the voice of the child,
And began to awake to life.

6. And Urizen, craving with hunger,
Stung with the odours of Nature,
Explor'd his dens around.

7. He form'd a line & a plummet
To divide the Abyss beneath;
He form'd a dividing rule.

8. He formed scales to weigh;
He formed massy weights;
He formed a brazen quadrant;
He formed golden compasses,
And began to explore the Abyss;
And he planted a garden of fruits.

9. But Los encircled Enitharmon
With fires of Prophecy
From the sight of Urizen & Orc.

10. And she bore an enormous race.

CHAP. VIII

1. Urizen explor'd his dens—
Mountain, moor, & wilderness,
With a globe of fire lighting his journey,
A fearful journey, annoy'd
By cruel enormities, forms

PLATE 23

Of life on his forsaken mountains.

2. And his world teem'd vast enormities,
Fright'ning, faithless, fawning
Portions of life, similitudes
Of a foot, or a hand, or a head,
Or a heart, or an eye; they swam, mischievous
Dread terrors, delighting in blood.

3. Most Urizen sicken'd to see
His eternal creations appear,
Sons & daughters of sorrow, on mountains,
Weeping! wailing! First Thiriel appear'd,
Astonish'd at his own existence,
Like a man from a cloud born; & Utha,
From the waters emerging, laments.
Grodna rent the deep earth, howling,
Amaz'd; his heavens immense cracks
Like the ground parch'd with heat. Then Fuzon
Flam'd out, first begotten, last born.
All his eternal sons in like manner;

His daughters from green herbs & cattle,
From monsters & worms of the pit.

4. He, in darkness clos'd, view'd all his race,
And his soul sicken'd! he curs'd
Both sons and daughters; for he saw
That no flesh nor spirit could keep
His iron laws one moment.

5. For he saw that Life liv'd upon death.

PLATE 25

The Ox in the slaughter house moans,
The Dog at the wintry door.
And he wept & he called it Pity,
And his tears flowed down on the winds.
6. Cold he wander'd on high, over their cities,
In weeping & pain & woe;
And wher-ever he wander'd in sorrows
Upon the aged heavens,
A cold shadow follow'd behind him
Like a spider's web, moist, cold & dim,
Drawing out from his sorrowing soul,
The dungeon-like heaven dividing,
Where ever the footsteps of Urizen
Walk'd over the cities in sorrow;

7. Till a Web, dark & cold, throughout all
The tormented element stretch'd
From the sorrows of Urizen's soul.
(And the Web is a Female in embrio.)
None could break the Web, no wings of fire,

8. So twisted the cords & so knotted
The meshes, twisted like to the human brain.

9. And all call'd it the Net of Religion.

CHAP. IX

1. Then the Inhabitants of those Cities
Felt their Nerves change into Marrow,
And hardening Bones began
In swift diseases and torments,

In throbbings & shootings & grindings
Thro' all the coasts; till weaken'd
The Senses inward rush'd, shrinking
Beneath the dark net of infection;

2. Till the shrunken eyes, clouded over,
Discern'd not the woven hypocrisy;
But the streaky slime in their heavens,
Brought together by narrowing perceptions,
Appear'd transparent air; for their eyes
Grew small like the eyes of a man,
And in reptile forms shrinking together
Of seven feet stature they remain'd.

3. Six days they shrunk up from existence,
And on the seventh day they rested,
And they bless'd the seventh day, in sick hope,
And forgot their eternal life.

4. And their thirty cities divided
In form of a human heart.
No more could they rise at will
In the infinite void, but bound down
To earth by their narrowing perceptions

PLATE 28

They lived a period of years,
Then left a noisome body
To the jaws of devouring darkness.

5. And their children wept & built
Tombs in the desolate places,
And form'd laws of prudence, and call'd them
The eternal laws of God.

6. And the thirty cities remain'd,
Surrounded by salt floods, now call'd
Africa: its name was then Egypt.

7. The remaining sons of Urizen
Beheld their brethren shrink together
Beneath the Net of Urizen.
Perswasion was in vain;

For the ears of the inhabitants
Were wither'd, & deafn'd & cold,
And their eyes could not discern
Their brethren of other cities.

8. So Fuzon call'd all together
The remaining children of Urizen,
And they left the pendulous earth:
They called it Egypt, & left it.

9. And the salt ocean rolled englob'd.

THE BOOK OF AHANIA

PLATE 2 CHAP. I

1. Fuzon, on a chariot iron-wing'd,
On spikd flames rose; his hot visage
Flam'd furious; sparkles his hair & beard
Shot down his wide bosom and shoulders.
On clouds of smoke rages his chariot,
And his right hand burns red in its cloud,
Moulding into a vast globe his wrath
As the thunder-stone is moulded,
Son of Urizen's silent burnings.

2. 'Shall we worship this Demon of smoke,'
Said Fuzon, 'this abstract non-entity,
This cloudy God seated on waters,
Now seen, now obscur'd, King of Sorrow?'

3. So he spoke, in a fiery flame,
On Urizen frowning indignant,
The Globe of wrath shaking on high.
Roaring with fury, he threw
The howling Globe; burning it flew,
Length'ning into a hungry beam. Swiftly

4. Oppos'd to the exulting flam'd beam
The broad Disk of Urizen upheav'd
Across the Void many a mile.

5. It was forg'd in mills where the winter
Beats incessant; ten winters the disk
Unremitting endur'd the cold hammer.

6. But the strong arm that sent it remember'd
The sounding beam; laughing it tore through
That beaten mass, keeping its direction,
The cold loins of Urizen dividing.

7. Dire shriek'd his invisible Lust.
Deep groan'd Urizen! stretching his awful hand,
Ahania (so name his parted soul)
He seiz'd on his mountains of Jealousy.
He groan'd, anguish'd, & called her Sin,
Kissing her and weeping over her;
Then hid her in darkness, in silence,
Jealous, tho' she was invisible.

8. She fell down, a faint shadow wand'ring
In chaos, and circling dark Urizen,
As the moon, anguish'd, circles the earth:
Hopeless! abhorr'd! a death-shadow,
Unseen, unbodied, unknown,
The mother of Pestilence.

9. But the fiery beam of Fuzon
Was a pillar of fire to Egypt,
Five hundred years wand'ring on earth,
Till Los seiz'd it and beat in a mass
With the body of the sun.

PLATE 3 **CHAP. II**

1. But the forehead of Urizen gathering,
And his eyes pale with anguish, his lips
Blue & changing, in tears and bitter
Contrition he prepar'd his Bow,

2. Form'd of Ribs, that in his dark solitude
When obscur'd in his forests fell monsters
Arose. For his dire Contemplations
Rush'd down like floods from his mountains,
In torrents of mud settling thick,
With Eggs of unnatural production

Forthwith hatching; some howl'd on his hills,
Some in vales, some aloft flew in air.

3. Of these, an enormous dread Serpent,
Scaled and poisonous horned,
Approach'd Urizen, even to his knees
As he sat on his dark rooted Oak.

4. With his horns he push'd furious
Great the conflict & great the jealousy
In cold poisons; but Urizen smote him.

5. First he poison'd the rocks with his blood;
Then polish'd his ribs, and his sinews
Dried; laid them apart till winter;
Then a Bow black prepar'd; on this Bow
A poisoned rock plac'd in silence.
He utter'd these words to the Bow:
6. 'O Bow of the clouds of secrecy,
O nerve of that lust form'd monster!
Send this rock swift, invisible thro'
The black clouds, on the bosom of Fuzon.'

7. So saying, in torment of his wounds,
He bent the enormous ribs slowly.
A circle of darkness!—then fixed
The sinew in its rest; then the Rock,
Poisonous source, plac'd with art, lifting difficult
Its weighty bulk; silent the rock lay,

8. While Fuzon, his tigers unloosing,
Thought Urizen slain by his wrath.
'I am God,' said he, 'eldest of things!'

9. Sudden sings the rock; swift & invisible
On Fuzon flew; enter'd his bosom.
His beautiful visage, his tresses
That gave light to the mornings of heaven
Were smitten with darkness, deform'd
And outstretch'd on the edge of the forest.

10. But the rock fell upon the Earth,
Mount Sinai in Arabia.

CHAP. III

1. The Globe shook; and Urizen, seated
On black clouds, his sore wound anointed
The ointment flow'd down on the void
Mix'd with blood—here the snake gets her poison.

2. With difficulty & great pain Urizen
Lifted on high the dead corse;
On his shoulders he bore it to where
A Tree hung over the Immensity.

3. For when Urizen shrunk away
From Eternals, he sat on a rock,
Barren, a rock which himself
From redounding fancies had petrified.
Many tears fell on the rock,
Many sparks of vegetation.
Soon shot the pained root
Of Mystery under his heel.
It grew a thick tree; he wrote
In silence his book of Iron;
Till the horrid plant, bending its boughs,
Grew to roots when it felt the earth.
And again sprung to many a tree.

4. Amaz'd started Urizen! when
He beheld himself compassed round
And high roofed over with trees.
He arose, but the stems stood so thick,
He with difficulty and great pain
Brought his Books, all but the Book

PLATE 4

Of Iron, from the dismal shade.

5. The Tree still grows over the Void,
Enrooting itself all around,
An endless labyrinth of woe!

6. The corse of his first begotten
On the accursed Tree of Mystery
On the topmost stem of this Tree
Urizen nail'd Fuzon's corse.

CHAP. IV

1. Forth flew the arrows of pestilence
Round the pale living Corse on the tree;

2. For in Urizen's slumbers of abstraction
In the infinite ages of Eternity,
When his Nerves of joy melted and flow'd
A white Lake on the dark blue air,
In perturb'd pain and dismal torment
Now stretching out, now swift conglobing,

3. Effluvia vapour'd above
In noxious clouds; these hover'd thick
Over the disorganiz'd Immortal,
Till petrific pain scurf'd o'er the Lakes
As the bones of man, solid & dark.

4. The clouds of disease hover'd wide
Around the Immortal in torment,
Perching around the hurtling bones
Disease on disease, shape on shape,
Winged, screaming in blood & torment.

5. The Eternal Prophet beat on his anvils,
Enrag'd in the desolate darkness;
He forg'd nets of iron around
And Los threw them around the bones.

6. The shapes, screaming, flutter'd vain;
Some combin'd into muscles & glands,
Some organs for craving and lust;
Most remain'd on the tormented void,
Urizen's army of horrors.

7. Round the pale living Corse on the Tree,
Forty years flew the arrows of pestilence.

8. Wailing and terror and woe
Ran thro' all his dismal world;
Forty years all his sons & daughters
Felt their skulls harden; then Asia
Arose in the pendulous deep.

9. They reptilize upon the Earth.

10. Fuzon groan'd on the Tree.

CHAP. V

1. The lamenting voice of Ahania,
Weeping upon the void
And round the Tree of Fuzon:
Distant in solitary night
Her voice was heard, but no form
Had she; but her tears from clouds
Eternal fell round the Tree;

2. And the voice cried: 'Ah, Urizen! Love!
Flower of morning! I weep on the verge
Of Non-entity; how wide the Abyss
Between Ahania and thee!

3. 'I lie on the verge of the deep,
I see thy dark clouds ascends,
I see thy black forests and floods,
A horrible waste to my eyes!

4. 'Weeping I walk over rocks,
Over dens, & thro' valleys of death.
Why didst thou despise Ahania,
To cast me from thy bright presence
Into the World of Loneness?

5. 'I cannot touch his hand,
Nor weep on his knees, nor hear
His voice & bow, nor see his eyes
And joy, nor hear his footsteps and
My heart leap at the lovely sound!
I cannot kiss the place
Whereon his bright feet have trod,

PLATE 5

But I wander on the rocks
With hard necessity.

6. 'Where is my golden palace?
Where my ivory bed?

Where the joy of my morning hour?
Where the sons of eternity singing

7. 'To awake bright Urizen, my king,
To arise to the mountain sport,
To the bliss of eternal valleys;

8. 'To awake my king in the morn
To embrace Ahania's joy
On the breath of his open bosom,
From my soft cloud of dew to fall
In showers of life on his harvests?

9. 'When he gave my happy soul
To the sons of eternal joy;
When he took the daughters of life
Into my chambers of love;

10. 'When I found babes of bliss on my beds,
And bosoms of milk in my chambers
Fill'd with eternal seed,
O! eternal births sung round Ahania
In interchange sweet of their joys.

11. 'Swell'd with ripeness & fat with fatness,
Bursting on winds, my odors,
My ripe figs and rich pomegranates
In infant joy at thy feet,
O Urizen, sported and sang.

12. 'Then thou with thy lap full of seed,
With thy hand full of generous fire,
Walked forth from the clouds of morning,
On the virgins of springing joy,
On the human soul to cast
The seed of eternal science.

13. 'The sweat poured down thy temples;
To Ahania return'd in evening
The moisture awoke to birth
My mother's-joys, sleeping in bliss.

14. 'But now, alone, over rocks, mountains,
Cast out from thy lovely bosom.

Cruel jealousy, selfish fear,
Self-destroying: how can delight
Renew in these chains of darkness,
Where bones of beasts are strown
On the bleak and snowy mountains,
Where bones from the birth are buried
Before they see the light?'

THE SONG OF LOS

Africa

PLATE 3

I will sing you a song of Los, the Eternal Prophet:
He sung it to four harps at the tables of Eternity.
In heart-formed Africa.
Urizen faded! Ariston shudder'd!
And thus the Song began:
ADAM stood in the garden of Eden
And Noah on the mountains of Ararat;
They saw Urizen give his Laws to the Nations
By the hands of the children of Los.
Adam shudder'd! Noah faded! black grew the sunny African
When Rintrah gave Abstract Philosophy to Brahma in the East.
(Night spoke to the Cloud:
'Lo, these Human form'd spirits, in smiling hypocrisy, War
Against one another; so let them War on, slaves to the eternal Elements.')
Noah shrunk beneath the waters;
Abram fled in fires from Chaldaea;
Moses beheld upon Mount Sinai forms of dark delusion.
To Trismegistus, Palamabron gave an abstract Law,
To Pythagoras, Socrates, & Plato.
Times rolled on o'er all the sons of Har; time after time
Orc on Mount Atlas howl'd, chain'd down with the Chain of Jealousy.

Then Oothoon hover'd over Judah & Jerusalem,
And Jesus heard her voice (a man of sorrows); he receiv'd
A Gospel from wretched Theotormon.
The human race began to wither, for the healthy built
Secluded places, fearing the joys of Love,
And the diseased only propagated.
So Antamon call'd up Leutha from her valleys of delight
And to Mahomet a loose Bible gave.
But in the North, to Odin, Sotha gave a Code of War,
Because of Diralada, thinking to reclaim his joy.

PLATE 4

These were the Churches, Hospitals, Castles, Palaces,
Like nets & gins & traps, to catch the joys of Eternity,
And all the rest a desart;
Till like a dream Eternity was obliterated & erased,
Since that dread day when Har and Heva fled,
Because their brethren & sisters liv'd in War & Lust;
And as they fled, they shrunk
Into two narrow doleful forms,
Creeping in reptile flesh upon
The bosom of the ground,
And all the vast of Nature shrunk
Before their shrunken eyes.

Thus the terrible race of Los & Enitharmon gave
Laws & Religions to the sons of Har, binding them more
And more to Earth, closing and restraining,
Till a Philosophy of Five Senses was complete:
Urizen wept & gave it into the hands of Newton & Locke.

Clouds roll heavy upon the Alps round Rousseau & Voltaire,
And on the mountains of Lebanon round the deceased Gods
Of Asia, & on the desarts of Africa round the Fallen Angels.
The Guardian Prince of Albion burns in his nightly tent.

Asia

PLATE 6

THE Kings of Asia heard
The howl rise up from Europe!
And each ran out from his Web,
From his ancient woven Den;
For the darkness of Asia was startled
At the thick-flaming, thought-creating fires of Orc.

And the Kings of Asia stood
And cried in bitterness of soul:

'Shall not the King call for Famine from the heath,
Nor the Priest for Pestilence from the fen?
To restrain! to dismay! to thin!
The inhabitants of mountain and plain,
In the day of full-feeding prosperity
And the night of delicious songs.

'Shall not the Councellor throw his curb
Of Poverty on the laborious?
To fix the price of labour,
To invent allegoric riches;

'And the privy admonishers of men
Call for fires in the City,
For heaps of smoking ruins,
In the night of prosperity & wantonness?

'To turn man from his path,
'To restrain the child from the womb,

PLATE 7

'To cut off the bread from the city,
That the remnant may learn to obey;

'That the pride of the heart may fail,
That the lust of the eyes may be quench'd,
That the delicate ear in its infancy
May be dull'd, and the nostrils clos'd up,
To teach mortal worms the path
That leads from the gates of the Grave.'

Urizen heard them cry,
And his shudd'ring waving wings
Went enormous above the red flames,
Drawing clouds of despair thro' the heavens
Of Europe as he went.
And his Books of brass, iron, & gold
Melted over the land as he flew,
Heavy-waving, howling, weeping.

And he stood over Judea,
And stay'd in his ancient place,
And stretch'd his clouds over Jerusalem.

For Adam, a mouldering skeleton,
Lay bleach'd on the garden of Eden;
And Noah, as white as snow
On the mountains of Ararat.

Then the thunders of Urizen bellow'd aloud
From his woven darkness above.

Orc, raging in European darkness,
Arose like a pillar of fire above the Alps,
Like a serpent of fiery flame!
    The sullen Earth
    Shrunk!
Forth from the dead dust rattling bones to bones
Join; shaking convuls'd, the shiv'ring clay breathes,
And all flesh naked stands: Fathers and Friends,
Mothers & Infants, Kings & Warriors.

The Grave shrieks with delight, & shakes
Her hollow womb, & clasps the solid stem,
Her bosom swells with wild desire,
And milk & blood & glandous wine
In rivers rush & shout & dance
On mountain, dale, and plain.

The Song of Los is Ended
  Urizen Wept.

LETTERS

I

A letter to Dr Trusler, dated 23 August 1799:

I really am sorry that you are fall'n out with the Spiritual World, Especially if I should have to answer for it. I feel very sorry that your Ideas & Mine on Moral Painting differ so much as to have made you angry with my method of Study. If I am wrong, I am wrong in good company?! I had hoped your plan comprehended All Species of this Art & Expecially that you would not reject that Species which gives Existence to Every other, namely, Visions of Eternity. You say that I want somebody to Elucidate my Ideas But you ought to know that What is Grand is necessarily obscure to Weak men. That which can be made Explicit to the Idiot is not worth my care. The wisest of the Ancients consider'd what is not too Explicit as the fittest for Instruction, because it rouzes the faculties to act .....

Fun I love, but too much Fun is of all things the most loathsom. Mirth is better than Fun, & Happiness is better than Mirth. I feel that a Man may be happy in This World. And I know that This World Is a World of imagination & Vision. I see Every thing I paint In This World, but Every body does not see alike. To the Eyes of a Miser a Guinea is more beautiful than the Sun, & a bag worn with the use of Money has more beautiful proportions than a Vine filled with Grapes. The tree which moves some to tears of joy is in the Eyes of others only a Green thing that stands in the way. Some See Nature all Ridicule & Deformity, & by these I shall not regulate my proportions; & Some Scarce see Nature at all. But to the Eyes of the Man of Imagination, Nature is Imagination itself. As a man is, So he Sees. As the Eye is formed, such are its Powers. You certainly Mistake, when you say that the Visions of Fancy are not to be found in This World. To Me This World is all One continued Vision of Fancy or Imagination, & I feel Flatter' d when I am told so. What is it sets Homer, Virgil & Milton in so high a rank of Art? Why is the Bible more Entertaining & Instructive than any other book? Is it not because they are addressed to the Imagination, which is Spiritual Sensation, & but mediately to the Understanding or Reason?

II

To my Friend Butts I write
My first Vision of Light:
On the yellow sands sitting,
The Sun was Emitting
His Glorious beams
From Heaven's high Streams.
Over Sea, over Land.
My eyes did Expand
Into regions of air
Away from all Care,
Into regions of fire
Remote from Desire.
The Light of the Morning
Heaven's Mountains adorning,
In particles bright
The jewels of Light
Distinct shone & clear.
Amaz'd & in fear
I each particle gazed,
Astonish'd, amazed;
For each was a Man
Human-form'd. Swift I ran,
For they beckon'd to me,
Remote by the Sea,
Saying: 'Each grain of Sand,
Every stone on the Land,
Each rock & each hill,
Each fountain & rill,
Each herb & each tree,
Mountain, hill, earth, & sea,
Cloud, Meteor & Star,
Are Men Seen Afar.'
I stood in the Streams
Of Heaven's bright beams.
And Saw Felpham sweet
Beneath my bright feet
In soft Female charms;

And here is Enitharmon's bower,
And Los the terrible thus hath sworn,
Because thou backward dost return,
Poverty, Envy, old age & fear
Shall bring thy Wife upon a bier,
And Butts shall give what Fuseli gave,
A dark black Rock & a gloomy Cave.'

I struck the Thistle with my foot,
And broke him up from his delving root
'Must the duties of life each other cross?
Must every joy be dung & dross?
Must my dear Butts feel cold neglect
Because I give Hayley his due respect?
Must Flaxman look upon me as wild,
And all my friends be with doubts beguil'd?
Must my Wife live in my Sister's bane,
Or my Sister survive on my Love's pain?
The curses of Los, the terrible shade,
And his dismal terrors make me afraid.'
So I spoke, & struck in my wrath
The old man weltering upon my path.
Then Los appear'd in all his power;
In the Sun he appear'd, descending before
My face in fierce flames. In my double sight
'Twas outward a Sun, inward Los in his might.

'My hands are labour'd day & night,
And Ease comes never in my sight.
My Wife has no indulgence given
Except what comes to her from Heaven.
We eat little, we drink less;
This Earth breeds not our happiness;
Another sun feeds our life's streams;
We are not warmed with thy beams.
Thou measurest not the Time to me,
Nor yet the Space that I do see;
My Mind is not with thy light array'd,
Thy Terrors shall not make me afraid.'
When I had my defiance given,

The Sun stood trembling in heaven;
The Moon, that glow'd remote below
Became leprous & white as snow;
And every soul of men on the Earth
Felt affliction, & sorrow, & sickness, & dearth.
Los flam'd in my path, & the Sun was hot
With the bows of my Mind & the arrows of Thought.
My bowstring fierce with ardour breathes,
My arrows glow in their golden sheaves;
My brothers & father march before;
The heavens drop with human gore.

Now I a fourfold vision see,
And a fourfold vision is given to me;
'Tis fourfold in my supreme delight,
And threefold in soft Beulah's night
And twofold Always, May God us keep
From single vision & Newton's sleep.

IV

O why was I born with a different face?
Why was I not born like the rest of my race?
When I look, each one starts! when I speak, I offend;
Then I'm silent & passive & lose every Friend.
Then my verse I dishonour, My pictures despise,
My person degrade, & my temper chastise;
And the pen is my terror, the pencil my shame;
All my Talents I bury, and dead is my Fame.

I am either too low or too highly prize'd;
When Elate I am Envy'd, When Meek I'm despis'd.

BLAKE'S NOTEBOOK
(C. 1802-4)

My Spectre around me night & day
Like a Wild beast guards my way;
My Emanation far within
Weeps incessantly for my Sin.

A Fathomless & boundless Deep,
There we wander, there we weep.
On the hungry craving wind
My Spectre follows thee behind.

He scents thy footsteps in the snow
Wheresoever thou dost go,
Thro' the wintry hail & rain:
When wilt thou return again?

Dost thou not in Pride & scorn
Fill with tempests all my morn?
And with jealousies & fears
Fill my pleasant nights with tears?

'Seven of my sweet loves thy knife
Has bereaved of their life;
Their marble tombs I built with tears,
And with cold & shuddering fears.

'Seven more loves weep night & day
Round the tombs where my loves lay,
And seven more loves attend each night
Around my couch with torches bright;

'And Seven more Loves in my bed
Crown with wine my mournful head,
Pitying & forgiving all
Thy transgressions great & small.

'When wilt thou return & view
My loves, & them to life renew?
When wilt thou return & live?
When wilt thou pity as I forgive?'

'Never, Never I return:
Still for Victory I burn!

Living, thee alone I'll have,
And when dead I'll be thy Grave.

'Thro' the Heav'n & Earth & Hell
Thou shalt never, never quell;
I will fly & thou pursue;
Night & morn the flight renew.'
'Till I turn from Female love
And root up the Infernal Grove,
I shall never worthy be
To Step into Eternity.
'And, to end thy cruel mocks
Annihilate thee on the rocks,
And another form create
To be subservient to my Fate.

'Let us agree to give up Love,
And root up the infernal grove;
Then shall we return & see
The worlds of happy Eternity.

'& Throughout all Eternity
I forgive you, you forgive me.
As our dear Redeemer said,
"This the Wine, & this the Bread."'

*

Mock on, Mock on, Voltaire, Rousseau!
Mock on, Mock on—'tis all in vain!
You throw the sand against the wind,
And the wind blows it back again.

And every sand becomes a Gem
Reflected in the beams divine;
Blown back they blind the mocking Eye,
But still in Israel's paths they shine.

The Atoms of Democritus
And Newton's Particles of Light
Are sands upon the Red sea shore,
Where Israel's tents do shine so bright.

Morning

To find the Western path,
Right thro' the Gates of Wrath
I urge my way.
Sweet Mercy leads me on
With soft repentant moan;
I see the break of day.

The war of swords & spears
Melted by dewy tears
Exhales on high;
The Sun is freed from fears
And with soft grateful tears
Ascends the sky.

THE PICKERING MS.

The Mental Traveller

I travel'd thro' a Land of Men,
A Land of Men & Women too;
And heard & saw such dreadful things
As cold Earth wanderers never knew.

For there the Babe is born in joy
That was begotten in dire woe
Just as we Reap in joy the fruit
Which we in bitter tears did sow.

And if the Babe is born a Boy
He's given to a Woman Old,
Who nails him down upon a rock,
Catches his shrieks in cups of gold.

She binds iron thorns around his head,
She pierces both his hands & feet,
She cuts his heart out at his side
To make it feel both cold & heat.

Her fingers number every Nerve,
Just as a Miser counts his gold;

She lives upon his shrieks & cries,
And she grows young as he grows old.

Till he becomes a bleeding youth,
And she becomes a Virgin bright;
Then he rends up his Manacles
And binds her down for his delight.

He plants himself in all her Nerves,
Just as a Husbandman his mould;
And she becomes his dwelling place
And Garden, fruitful seventy fold.

And Aged Shadow soon he fades,
Wand'ring round an Earthly Cot,
Full filled all with gems & gold
Which he by industry had got.

And these are the gems of the Human Soul:
The rubies & pearls of a lovesick eye,
The countless gold of the akeing heart,
The martyr's groan & the lover's sigh.

They are his meat, they are his drink;
He feeds the Beggar & the Poor
And the wayfaring Traveller;
For ever open is his door.

His grief is their eternal joy;
They make the roofs & walls to ring;
Till from the fire on the hearth
A little Female Babe does spring.

And she is all of solid fire
And gems & gold, that none his hand
Dares stretch to touch her Baby form,
Or wrap her in his swaddling-band.

But She comes to the Man she loves,
If young or old, or rich or poor;
They soon drive out the Aged Host,
A Beggar at another's door.

He wanders weeping far away
Untill some other take him in;

Oft blind & age-bent, sore distrest,
Until he can a Maiden win.

And to allay his freezing Age
The Poor Man takes her in his arms;
The Cottage fades before his sight,
The Garden & its lovely Charms;

The Guests are scatter'd thro' the land,
For the Eye altering alters all;
The Senses roll themselves in fear,
And the flat Earth becomes a Ball;

The Stars, Sun, Moon, all shrink away—
A desert vast without a bound,
And nothing left to eat or drink,
And a dark desart all around.

The honey of her Infant lips,
The bread & wine of her sweet smile,
The wild game of her roving eye,
Does him to Infancy beguile.

For as he eats & drinks he grows
Younger & younger every day;
And on the desart wild they both
Wander in terror & dismay.

Like the wild Stag she flees away,
Her fear plants many a thicket wild;
While he pursues her night & day,
By various arts of Love beguil'd;

By various arts of Love and Hate
Till the wide desart planted o'er
With Labyrinths of wayward Love,
Where roam the Lion, Wolf, & Boar;

Till he becomes a wayward Babe,
And she a weeping Woman Old.
Then many a Lover wanders here,
The Sun and Stars are nearer roll'd,

The trees bring forth sweet Extasy
To all who in the desart roam,

Till many a City There is Built,
And many a pleasant shepherd's home.

But when they find the frowning Babe,
Terror strikes thro' the region wide;
They cry 'the Babe! the Babe is born!'
And flee away on every side.

For who dare touch the frowning form,
His arm is wither'd to its root;
Lions, boars, wolves, all howling flee,
And every tree does shed its fruit,

And none can touch that frowning form,
Except it be a Woman Old;
She nails him down upon the Rock,
And all is done as I have told.

The Crystal Cabinet

The Maiden caught me in the Wild,
Where I was dancing merrily;
She put me into her Cabinet,
And Lock'd me up with a golden Key.

This Cabinet is form'd of Gold
And Pearl & Crystal shining bright,
And within it opens into a World
And a little lovely Moony Night.

Another England there I saw,
Another London with its Tower,
Another Thames & other Hills,
And another pleasant Surrey Bower,

Another Maiden like herself,
Translucent, lovely, shining clear,
Threefold each in the other clos'd—
O, what a pleasant trembling fear!

O, what a smile! a threefold Smile
Fill'd me, that like a flame I burn'd.
I bent to Kiss the lovely Maid,
And found a Threefold Kiss return'd.

I strove to seize the inmost Form
With ardor fierce & hands of flame,
But burst the Crystal Cabinet
And like a Weeping Babe became,

A weeping Babe upon the wild,
And weeping Woman, pale, reclin'd,
And in the outward air again
I fill'd with woes the passing Wind.

Auguries of Innocence

To see a World in a Grain of Sand
And a Heaven in a Wild Flower,
Hold Infinity in the palm of your hand
And Eternity in an hour.

A Robin Redbreast in a Cage
Puts all Heaven in a Rage.
A dove house fill'd with doves & Pigeons
Shudders Hell thro' all its regions.
A Dog starv'd at his Master's Gate
Predicts the ruin of the State.
A Horse misus'd upon the Road
Calls to Heaven for Human Blood.
Each outcry of the hunted Hare
A fibre from the Brain does tear.
A Skylark wounded in the wing,
A Cherubim does cease to sing.
The Game Cock clip'd & arm'd for fight
Does the Rising Sun affright.
Every Wolf's & Lion's howl
Raises from Hell a Human Soul.
The wild deer wand'ring here & there,
Keeps the Human Soul from Care.
The Lamb misus'd breeds Public strife,
And yet forgives the Butcher's Knife.
The Bat that flits at close of Eve
Has left the Brain that won't Believe.
The Owl that calls upon the Night

Speaks the Unbeliever's fright.
He who shall hurt the little Wren
Shall never be belov'd by Men.
He who the Ox to wrath has mov'd
Shall never be by Woman lov'd.
The wanton Boy that kills the Fly
Shall feel the Spider's enmity.
He who torments the Chafer's sprite
Weaves a Bower in endless Night.
The Catterpiller on the Leaf
Repeats to thee thy mother's grief.
Kill not the moth nor butterfly,
For the last Judgment draweth nigh.
He who shall train the Horse to war
Shall never pass the Polar Bar.
The beggar's Dog & Widow's cat,
Feed them, & thou wilt grow fat.
The Gnat that sings his Summer's song
Poison gets from Slander's tongue
The poison of the Snake & newt
Is the sweat of Envy's foot.
The Poison of the Honey Bee
Is the Artist's Jealousy.
The Prince's Robes & Beggar's Rags
Are Toadstools on the Miser's Bags.
A truth that's told with bad intent
Beats all the Lies you can invent.
It is right it should be so;
Man was made for Joy & Woe,
And when this we rightly know,
Thro' the World we safely go.
Joy and woe are woven fine,
A Clothing for the Soul divine;
Under every grief & pine
Runs a joy with silken twine.
The Babe is more than swaddling Bands;
Throughout all these Human Lands
Tools were made, & Born were hands—

Every Farmer Understands.
Every Tear from Every Eye
Becomes a Babe in Eternity;
This is caught by Females bright
And return'd to its own delight.
The Bleat, the Bark, Bellow & oar
Are Waves that Beat on Heaven's Shore.
The Babe that weeps the rod beneath
Writes 'Reveng' in realms of death.
The Beggar's Rags, fluttering in Air
Does to Rags the Heavens tear.
The Soldier, arm'd with Sword & Gun,
Palsied strikes the Summer's Sun.
The poor Man's Farthing is worth more
Than all the Gold on Afric's Shore.
One Mite wrung from the Lab'rer's hands
Shall buy & sell the Miser's Lands;
Or if protected from on high
Does that whole Nation sell & buy.
He who mocks the Infant's Faith
Shall be mock'd in Age & Death.
He who shall teach the Child to Doubt
The rotting Grave shall ne'er get out.
He who respects the Infant's faith
Triumphs over Hell & Death.
The child's toys & the Old Man's Reasons
Are the Fruits of the Two seasons.
The Questioner who sits so sly
Shall never know how to Reply.
He who replies to words of Doubt
Doth put the Light of Knowledge out.
The Strongest Poison ever known
Came from Cæsar's Laurel Crown.
Nought can deform the Human Race
Like to the Armour's iron brace.
When Gold & Gems adorn the plow
To peaceful Arts shall Envy Bow.
A Riddle, or the Cricket's Cry,

Is to Doubt a fit Reply.
The Emmet's Inch & eagle's Mile
Make Lame Philosophy to smile.
He who Doubts from what he sees
Will ne'er Believe, do what you please.
If the Sun & Moon should doubt,
They'd immediately Go out.
To be in a Passion you Good may do,
But no Good if a Passion is in you.
The Whore & Gambler, by the State
Licenc'd, build that Nation's Fate.
The harlot's cry from Street to Street
Shall weave Old England's winding Sheet
The Winner's Shout, the Loser's Curse,
Dance before dead England's Hearse.
Every Night & every Morn
Some to Misery are Born.
Every Morn & every Night
Some are Born to sweet delight.
Some are Born to sweet delight,
Some are Born to Endless Night.
We are led to Believe a Lie
When we see not Thro' the Eye,
Which was Born in a Night to perish in a Night,
When the Soul Slept in Beams of Light.
God Appears, & God is Light
To those poor Souls who dwell in Night,
But does a Human Form Display
To those who Dwell in Realms of Day.

THE FOUR ZOAS

NIGHT 1

Four Mighty Ones are in every Man. A Perfect Unity
Cannot Exist but from the Universal Brotherhood of Eden
The Universal Man, to Whom be Glory Evermore, Amen.
What are the Natures of those Living Creatures the Heavenly Father only
Knoweth; no Individual Knoweth nor Can know in all Eternity.

Los was the fourth immortal starry one, & in the Earth
Of a bright Universe Empery attended day & night,
Days & nights of revolving joy. Urthona was his name
In Eden. In the Auricular Nerves of Human life,
Which is the Earth of Eden, he his Emanations propagated,
Fairies of Albion, afterwards Gods of the Heathen. Daughter of Beulah, Sing
His fall into Division & his Resurrection to Unity.

* * *

NIGHT 1

'Hear! I will sing a Song of Death; it is a Song of Vala!
The Fallen Man takes his repose; Urizen sleeps in the porch.
Luvah and Vala woke, and flew up from the Human Heart
Into the Brain; from thence upon the pillow Vala slumber'd.
And Luvah siez'd the Horses of Light, & rose into the Chariot of Day.

* * *

NIGHT 2

'What is the price of Experience? do men buy it for a song,
Or wisdom for a dance in the street? No, it is bought with the price
Of all that a man hath—his house, his wife, his children.
Wisdom is sold in the desolate market where none come to buy,
And in the wither'd field where the farmer plows for bread in vain.

It is an easy thing to triumph in the summer's sun
And in the vintage, & to sing on the waggon loaded with corn;
It is an easy thing to talk of patience to the afflicted
To speak the laws of prudence to the houseless wanderer,
To listen to the hungry ravens' cry in wintry season
When the red blood is fill'd with wine & with the marrow of lambs;
It is an easy thing to laugh at wrathful elements,
To hear the dog howl at the wintry door, the ox in the slaughter house moan,
To see a god on every wind, & a blessing on every blast
To hear sounds of love in the thunderstorm that destroys our enemy's house
To rejoice in the blight that covers his field, & the sickness that cuts off his children,
While our olive & vine sing & laugh round our door & our children bring fruits & flowers.
Then the groan & the dolor are quite forgotten, & the slave grinding at the mill,
And the captive in chains, & the poor in the prison, & the soldier in the field
When the shatter'd bone hath laid him groaning among the happier dead.
It is an easy thing to rejoice in the tents of prosperity;
Thus could I sing & thus rejoice, but it is not so with me!

* * *

NIGHT 3

'Then, O my dear lord, listen to Ahania, listen to the vision,
The vision of Ahania in the slumbers of Urizen,
When Urizen slept in the porch and the Ancient Man was smitten.
The Darkning Man walk'd on the steps of fire before his halls,
And Vala walk'd with him in dreams of soft deluding slumber.
He looked up & saw thee, Prince of Light, thy splendor faded,
But saw not Los nor Enitharmon for Luvah hid them in shadow,
In a soft cloud Outstretch'd across; and Luvah dwelt in the cloud.

Then Man ascended mourning into the splendors of his palace;
Above him rose a Shadow from his wearied intellect
Of living gold, pure, perfect, holy; in white linen pure he hover'd,
A sweet. entrancing self delusion, a watry vision of Man.
Soft exulting in existence, all the Man absorbing.
Man fell upon his face prostrate before the watry shadow
Saying 'O Lord, whence is this change? Thou knowest I am nothing'.
And Vala trembled & coverd her face, & her locks were spread on the pavement.
I heard, astonishd at the Vision, & my heart trembled within me;
I heard the voice of the Slumberous Man, and thus he spoke
Idolatrous to his own Shadow, words of Eternity uttering,
"O, I am nothing when I enter into judgment with thee.
If thou withdraw thy breath, I die & vanish into Hades;
If thou dost lay thine hand upon me, behold I am silent;
If thou withhold thine hand, I perish like a fallen leaf.
O, I am nothing, & to nothing must return again;
If thou withdraw thy breath, behold I am oblivion."'

NIGHT 4

For Urizen beheld the terrors of the Abyss, wand'ring among
The ruin'd spirits, once his children & the children of Luvah.
Scar'd at the sound of their own sigh that seems to shake the immense
They wander Moping, in their heart a Sun, a Dreary moon,
A Universe of fiery constellations in their brain
An Earth of wintry woe beneath their feet, & round their loins
Waters or winds or clouds or brooding lightnings & pestilential plagues.
Beyond the bounds of their own self their senses cannot penetrate:
As the tree knows not what is outside of its leaves & bark
And yet it drinks the summer joy & fears the winter sorrow,
So in the regions of the grave none knows his dark compeer,
Tho' he partakes of his dire woes & mutual returns the pang,
The throb, the dolor, the convulsion in soul-sickening woes...

Then came he among fiery cities & castles built of burning steel.
Then he beheld the forms of tygers & of Lions, dishumaniz'd men.
Many in serpents & in worms stretch'd out enormous length
Over the sullen mould, & slimy tracks obstruct his way,
Drawn out from deep, to deep woven by ribb'd
And scaled monsters, or arm'd in iron shell or shell of brass
Or gold, a glittering torment shining & hissing in eternal pain
Some, columns of fire or of water, sometimes stretch'd out in height,
Sometimes in length, sometimes englobing wandering in vain, seeking for ease.
His voice to them was but an inarticulate thunder, for their Ears
Were heavy & dull, & their eyes & nostrils closed up.
Oft he stood by a howling victim, Questioning in words
Soothing or Furious no one answer'd every one wrap'd up
In his own sorrow howl'd regardless of his words, nor voice
Of sweet response could he obtain tho' oft assay'd with tears.
He knew they were his Children ruin'd in his ruin'd world
Oft would he stand & question a fierce scorpion glowing with gold;
In vain: the terror heard not; then a lion he would Sieze
By the fierce mane, staying his howling course; in vain the voice.
Of Urizen, vain the Eloquent tongue. A Rock, a Cloud, a Mountain,
Were now not Vocal as in Climes of happy Eternity
Where the lamb replies to the infant voice & the lion to the man of years,
Giving them sweet instructions; Where the Cloud, the River & the Field
Talk with the husbandman & shepherd. But these attack'd him sore,
Siezing upon his feet & rending the Sinews, that in Caves
He hid to recure his obstructed powers with rest & oblivion.
Here he had time enough to repent of his rashly threaten'd curse.

·izen spoke. He shook his snows from off his Shoulders &

ı a Pyramid of mist, his white robes scattering
leecy white; renew'd, he shook his aged mantles off
he fires. Then glorious, bright, Exulting in his joy,
ounding rose into the heavens in naked majesty,
liant Youth.

*   *   *

He saw them curs'd beyond his Curse; his soul melted with fear.
He could not take their fetters off, for they grew from the soul.
Nor could he quench the fires, for they flamd out from the heart
Nor could he calm the Elements, because himself was Subject.
So he threw his flight in terror & pain, & in repentant tears.

NIGHT 7

And Urizen Read in his book of brass in sounding tonest:
'Listen, O Daughters, to my voice, Listen to the Words of Wisdom.
So shall you govern over all. Let Moral Duty tune your tongue
But be your hearts harder than the nether millstone.
To bring the shadow of Enitharmon beneath our wondrous tree
That Los may Evaporate like smoke & be no more,
Draw down Enitharmon to the Spectre of Urthona
And let him have dominion over Los the terrible shade.
Compell the poor to live upon a Crust of bread by soft mild arts.
Smile when they frown, frown when they smile; & when a man looks pale
With labour & abstinence, say he looks healthy & happy
And when his children sicken, let them die—there are enough
Born even too many, & our Earth will be overrun
Without these arts. If you would make the poor live with temper.
With pomp give every crust of bread you give; with gracious cunning
Magnify small gifts; reduce the man to want a gift & then give with pomp.
Say he smiles if you hear him sigh. If pale, say he is ruddy.
Preach temperance: say he is overgorg'd & drowns his wit
In strong drink. tho' you know that bread & water are all
He can afford. Flatter his wife pity his children, till we can
Reduce all to our will, as spaniels are taught with art.
Lo, how the heart & brain are formed in the breeding womb

Of Enitharmon! how it buds with life & forms the bones,
The little heart, the liver & the red blood in its labyrinths!
By gratified desire, by strong devouring appetite, she fills
Los with ambitious fury that his race shall all devour.'
Then Orc cried: 'Curse thy Cold hypocrisy! Already round thy tree
In scales that shine with gold & rubies thou beginnest to weaken
My divided Spirit. Like a worm I rise in peace, unbound
From wrath. Now when I rage, my fetters bind me more.
O torment! O torment! A Worm compelld! Am I a worm?
Is it in strong deceit that man is born? In strong deceit
Thou dost restrain my fury, that the worm may fold the tree.
Avaunt, Cold hypocrite! I am chain'd or thou couldst not use me thus;
The Man shall rage, bound with this Chain; the worm in silence creep.
Thou wilt not cease from rage. Grey Demon, silence all thy storms;
Give me example of thy mildness, King of furious hail storms.
Art thou the cold attractive power that holds me in this chain
I well remember how I stole thy light & it became fire
Consuming. Thou Know'st me now O Urizen, Prince of Light;
And I know thee. Is this the triumph, this the Godlike State
That lies beyond the bounds of Science in the Grey obscure?'
Terrified Urizen heard Orc, now certain that he was Luvah
And Orc began to Organize a Serpent body,
Despising Urizen's light & turning it into flaming fire,
Recieving as a poison'd Cup Recieves the heavenly wine,
And turning affection into fury & thought into abstractiont,
A Self-consuming dark devourer rising into the heavens.
Urizen, envious, brooding, sat, & saw the secret terror
Flame high in pride & laugh to scorn the source of his deceit,
Nor knew the source of his own, but thought himself the Sole author
Of all his wandering Experiments in the horrible Abyss.
He knew that weakness stretches out in breadth & length; he knew

That wisdom reaches high & deep; and the
In Serpent form compel'd, stretch out & up
He suffer'd him to Climb that he might dr
Into submission to his will; nor knew the

* * *

NIGHT 9

Urizen wept in the dark deep, anxious hi
To reassume the human; & he wept in th
Saying: 'O that I had never drank the wir
Of dark mortality, nor cast my view into
My back dark'ning the present, clouding
And building arches high, & cities, t domes
Whose smoke destroy'd the pleasant gar Kennels
Chok'd the bright rivers, burd'ning wit deep;
Thro' Chaos seeking for delight, & in sp
Seeking the Eternal which is always pre
Seeking for pleasure which unsought path
And on the fleeces of mild flocks who
But I, the labourer of ages, whose unw
Are thus deform'd with hardness, wit spear
And with the Chisel & the mallet, I, w
Order the nations, separating family b
Alone enjoy not. I alone, in misery su
Ungratified give all my joy unto this I
Then Go, O dark futuriy! I will cast th
Heavens of my brain, nor will I look
Which I have made; for lo, futurity is
Let Orc consume, let Tharmas rage, l
All strength to Los & Enitharmon, &
Rend down this fabric, as a wall ruir
Rage, Orc! Rage, Tharmas! Urizen n

He saw them curs'd beyond his Curse; his soul melted with fear.
He could not take their fetters off, for they grew from the soul.
Nor could he quench the fires, for they flamd out from the heart
Nor could he calm the Elements, because himself was Subject.
So he threw his flight in terror & pain, & in repentant tears.

NIGHT 7

And Urizen Read in his book of brass in sounding tonest:
'Listen, O Daughters, to my voice, Listen to the Words of Wisdom.
So shall you govern over all. Let Moral Duty tune your tongue
But be your hearts harder than the nether millstone.
To bring the shadow of Enitharmon beneath our wondrous tree
That Los may Evaporate like smoke & be no more,
Draw down Enitharmon to the Spectre of Urthona
And let him have dominion over Los the terrible shade.
Compell the poor to live upon a Crust of bread by soft mild arts.
Smile when they frown, frown when they smile; & when a man looks pale
With labour & abstinence, say he looks healthy & happy
And when his children sicken, let them die—there are enough
Born even too many, & our Earth will be overrun
Without these arts. If you would make the poor live with temper.
With pomp give every crust of bread you give; with gracious cunning
Magnify small gifts; reduce the man to want a gift & then give with pomp.
Say he smiles if you hear him sigh. If pale, say he is ruddy.
Preach temperance: say he is overgorg'd & drowns his wit
In strong drink. tho' you know that bread & water are all
He can afford. Flatter his wife pity his children, till we can
Reduce all to our will, as spaniels are taught with art.
Lo, how the heart & brain are formed in the breeding womb

Of Enitharmon! how it buds with life & forms the bones,
The little heart, the liver & the red blood in its labyrinths!
By gratified desire, by strong devouring appetite, she fills
Los with ambitious fury that his race shall all devour.'
Then Orc cried: 'Curse thy Cold hypocrisy! Already round thy tree
In scales that shine with gold & rubies thou beginnest to weaken
My divided Spirit. Like a worm I rise in peace, unbound
From wrath. Now when I rage, my fetters bind me more.
O torment! O torment! A Worm compelld! Am I a worm?
Is it in strong deceit that man is born? In strong deceit
Thou dost restrain my fury, that the worm may fold the tree.
Avaunt, Cold hypocrite! I am chain'd or thou couldst not use me thus;
The Man shall rage, bound with this Chain; the worm in silence creep.
Thou wilt not cease from rage. Grey Demon, silence all thy storms;
Give me example of thy mildness, King of furious hail storms.
Art thou the cold attractive power that holds me in this chain
I well remember how I stole thy light & it became fire
Consuming. Thou Know'st me now O Urizen, Prince of Light;
And I know thee. Is this the triumph, this the Godlike State
That lies beyond the bounds of Science in the Grey obscure?'
Terrified Urizen heard Orc, now certain that he was Luvah
And Orc began to Organize a Serpent body,
Despising Urizen's light & turning it into flaming fire,
Recieving as a poison'd Cup Recieves the heavenly wine,
And turning affection into fury & thought into abstractiont,
A Self-consuming dark devourer rising into the heavens.

Urizen, envious, brooding, sat, & saw the secret terror
Flame high in pride & laugh to scorn the source of his deceit,
Nor knew the source of his own, but thought himself the Sole author
Of all his wandering Experiments in the horrible Abyss.
He knew that weakness stretches out in breadth & length; he knew

That wisdom reaches high & deep; and therefore he made Orc,
In Serpent form compel'd, stretch out & up the mysterious tree.
He suffer'd him to Climb that he might draw all human forms
Into submission to his will; nor knew the dread result.

* * *

NIGHT 9

Urizen wept in the dark deep, anxious his Scaly form
To reassume the human; & he wept in the dark deep
Saying: 'O that I had never drank the wine nor eat the bread
Of dark mortality, nor cast my view into futurity, nor turn'd
My back dark'ning the present, clouding with a cloud,
And building arches high, & cities, turrets & towers and domes
Whose smoke destroy'd the pleasant gardens & whose running Kennels
Chok'd the bright rivers, burd'ning with my Ships the angry deep;
Thro' Chaos seeking for delight, & in spaces remote,
Seeking the Eternal which is always present to the wise,
Seeking for pleasure which unsought falls round the infant's path
And on the fleeces of mild flocks who neither care nor labour.
But I, the labourer of ages, whose unwearied hands
Are thus deform'd with hardness, with the sword & with the spear
And with the Chisel & the mallet, I, whose labours vast
Order the nations, separating family by family.
Alone enjoy not. I alone, in misery supreme.
Ungratified give all my joy unto this Luvah & Vala.
Then Go, O dark futuriy! I will cast thee forth from these
Heavens of my brain, nor will I look upon that void
Which I have made; for lo, futurity is in this moment!
Let Orc consume, let Tharmas rage, let dark Urthona give
All strength to Los & Enitharmon, & let Los self-curs'd
Rend down this fabric, as a wall ruin'd & family extinct
Rage, Orc! Rage, Tharmas! Urizen no longer curbs your rage'.

So Urizen spoke. He shook his snows from off his Shoulders & arose
As on a Pyramid of mist, his white robes scattering
The fleecy white; renew'd, he shook his aged mantles off
Into the fires. Then glorious, bright, Exulting in his joy,
He sounding rose into the heavens in naked majesty,
In radiant Youth.

* * *

MILTON

Preface

PLATE 1

...
And did those feet in ancient time
Walk upon England's mountains green?
And was the holy Lamb of God
On England's pleasant pastures seen?

And did the Countenance Divine
Shine forth upon our clouded hills?
And was Jerusalem builded here
Among these dark Satanic Mills?

Bring me my Bow of burning gold;
Bring me my Arrows of desire;
Bring me my Spear; O clouds unfold!
Bring me my Chariot of fire!

I will not cease from Mental Fight,
Nor shall my Sword sleep in my hand,
Till we have built Jerusalem
In England's green & pleasant Land.

Would to God that all the Lord's people were Prophets.
Numbers XI. 29

Book the First

PLATE 2

Daughters of Beulah! Muses who inspire the Poet's Song,
Record the journey of immortal Milton thro' your Realms
Of terror & mild moony lustre, in soft sexual delusions
Of varied beauty, to delight the wanderer and repose
His burning thirst & freezing hunger! Come into my hand
By your mild power, descending down the Nerves of my right
arm

From out the Portals of my Brain, where by your ministry
The Eternal Great Humanity Divine planted his Paradise,
And in it caus'd the Spectres of the Dead to take sweet forms
In likeness of himself. Tell also of the False Tongue! vegetated
Beneath your land of shadows of its sacrifices and
Its offerings, even till Jesus, the image of the Invisible God,
Became its prey—a curse, an offering and an atonement
For Death Eternal in the heavens of Albion, & before the Gates
Of Jerusalem his Emanation, in the heavens beneath Beulah.
Say first ! what mov'd Milton, who walk'd about in Eternity
One hundred years, pond'ring the intricate mazes of Providence,
Unhappy tho' in heav'n—he obey'd, he murmur'd not, he was silent
Viewing his Sixfold Emanation scatter'd thro' the deep
In torment—To go into the deep, her to redeem & himself perish?
What cause at length mov'd Milton to this unexampled deed?
A Bard's prophetic Song! for sitting at eternal tables,
Terrific among the Sons of Albion, in chorus solemn & loud,
A Bard broke forth! all sat attentive to the awful man.

* * *

PLATE 14

Then Milton rose up from the heavens of Albion ardorous.
The whole Assembly wept prophetic, seeing in Milton's face
And in his lineaments divine the shades of Death & Ulro.
He took of the robe of the promise, & ungirded himself from the oath of God.
And Milton said: 'I go to Eternal Death! The Nations still
Follow after the detestable Gods of Priam, in pomp
Of warlike selfhood, contradicting and blaspheming.
When will the Resurredtion come to deliver the sleeping body
From corruptibility? O when, Lord Jesus, wilt thou come?
Tarry no longer, for my soul lies at the gates of death.
I will arise and look forth for the morning of the grave;
I will go down to the sepulcher to see if morning breaks;
I will go down to self annihilation and eternal death;

Lest the Last Judgment come & find me unannihilate,
And I be seiz'd & giv'n into the hands of my own Selfhood.
The Lamb of God is seen thro' mists & shadows, hov'ring
Over the sepulchers in clouds of Jehovah & winds of Elohim,
A disk of blood, distant; & heav'ns & earths roll dark between.
What do I here before the Judgment? without my Emanation?
With the daughters of memory & not with the daughters of inspiration?
I in my Selfhood am that Satan; I am that Evil One!
He is my Spectre! In my obedience to loose him from my Hells,
To claim the Hells, my Furnaces, I go to Eternal Death.'

* * *

PLATE 21

But Milton entering my Foot, I saw in the nether
Regions of the Imagination—also all men on Earth
And all in Heaven saw in the nether regions of the Imagination
In Ulro beneath Beulah—the vast breach of Milton's descent.
But I knew not that it was Milton, for man cannot know
What passes in his members till periods of Space & Time
Reveal the secrets of Eternity; for more extensive
Than any other earthly things are Man's earthly lineaments.

And all this Vegetable World appear'd on my left Foot,
As a bright sandal form'd immortal of precious stones & gold :
I stooped down & bound it on to walk forward thro' Eternity.

* * *

PLATE 22

...what time I bound my sandals
On to walk forward thro' Eternity, Los descended to me;
And Los behind me stood, a terrible flaming Sun, just close
Behind my back. I turned round in terror, and behold!
Los stood in that fierce glowing fire, & he also stoop'd down
And bound my sandals on in Udan-Adan. Trembling I stood
Exceedingly with fear & terror, standing in the Vale
Of Lambeth; but he kissed me, and wish'd me health,
And I became One Man with him arising in my strength.

'Twas too late now to recede. Los had enter'd into my soul;
his terrors now posses'd me whole! I arose in fury & strength.
'I am that Shadowy Prophet who Six Thousand Years ago
Fell from my station in the Eternal bosom. Six Thousand Years
Are finish'd. I return! both Time & Space obey my will.
I in Six Thousand Years walk up and down; for not one Moment
Of Time is lost, nor one Event of Space unpermanent,
But all remain; every fabric of Six Thousand Years
Remains permanent. Tho' on the Earth where Satan
Fell and was cut off all things vanish & are seen no more,
They vanish not from me & mine; we guard them first & last.
The generations of men run on in the tide of Time,
But leave their destin'd lineaments permanent for ever & ever.'

* * *

PLATE 24

Los is by mortals nam'd Time; Enitharmon is nam'd Space.
But they depict him bald & aged who is in eternal youth,
All powerful, and his locks flourish like the brows of morning.
He is the Spirit of Prophecy, the ever apparent Elias.
Time is the mercy of Eternity; without Time's swiftness,
Which is the swiftest of all things, all were eternal torment.
All the Gods of the Kingdoms of Earth labour in Los's Halls:
Every one is a fallen Son of the Spirit of Prophecy;
He is the Fourth Zoa, that stood around the Throne Divine.

* * *

PLATE 25

Thou seest the Constellations in the deep & wondrous Night;
They rise in order and countinue their immortal courses
Upon the mountains & in vales, with harp & heavenly song,
With flute & clarion, with cups & measures fill'd with foaming wine.
Glitt'ring the streams reflect the Vision of beatitude,
And the calm Ocean joys beneath & smooths his awful waves.

PLATE 26

These are the Sons of Los, & these the Labourers of the Vintage.
Thou seest the gorgeous clothed Flies that dance & sport in summer
Upon the sunny brooks & meadows; every one the dance
Knows in its intricate mazes of delight artful to weave,
Each one to sound his instruments of music in the dace,
To touch each other & recede, to cross & change & return.
These are the Children of Los. Thou seest the Trees on mountains;
The wind blows heavy, loud they thunder thro' the darksome sky,
Uttering prophecies & speaking instructive words to the sons
Of men. These are the Sons of Los, these the Visions of Eternity;
But we see only as it were the hem of their garments
When with our vegetable eyes we view these wondrous Visions.
...
And every Generated Body in its inward form
Is a garden of delight & a building of magnificence,
Built by the Sons of Los in Bowlahoola & Allamanda;
And the herbs & flowers & furniture & beds &chambers
Continually woven in the Looms of Enitharmon's Daughters,
In bright Cathedron's golden Dome with care & love & tears.
For the various Classes of Men are all mark'd out determinate
In Bowlahoola, & as the Spectres choose their affinities
So they are born on Earth, & every Class is determinate;
But not by Natural, but by Spiritual power alone, Because
The Natural power continually seeks & tends to Destruction,
Ending in Death, which would of itself be Eternal Death.
And all are Class'd by Spiritual & not by Natural power,

And every Neutral Effect has a Spiritual Cause, and Not
A Natural; for a Natural Cause only seems: it is a Delusion
Of Ulro, & a ratio of the perishing Vegetable Memory.

* * *

PLATE 28

But others of the Sons of Los build Moments & Minutes & Hours
And Days & Months & Years & Ages & Periods, wondrous buildings;
And every Moment has a Couch of gold for soft repose,
(A Moment equals a pulsation of the artery),
And between every two Moments stands a Daughter of Beulah
To feed the Sleepers on their Couches with maternal care.
And Every Minute has an azure Tent with silken Veils;
And Every Hour has a bright golden Gate carved with skill;
And every Day & Night has Walls of brass & Gates of adamant,
Shining like precious stones & ornamented with appropriate signs;
And every Month a silver paved Terrace builded high;
And every Year invulnerable Barriers with high Towers;
And every Age is Moated deep with Bridges of silver & gold;
And every Seven Ages is Incircled with a Flaming Fire.
Now Seven Ages is amounting to Two Hundred Years:
Each has its Guard, each Moment, Minute, Hour, Day, Month & Year.
All are the work of Fairy hands of the Four Elements.
The Guard are Angels of Providence on duty evermore.
Every Time less than a pulsation of the artery
Is equal in its period & value to Six Thousand Years;

PLATE 29

For in this Period the Poet's work is Done, and all the Great
Events of Time start forth & are conciev'd in such a Period,
Within a Moment, a Pulsation of the Artery.

The Sky is an immortal Tent built by the Sons of Los;
And every Space that a Man views around his dwelling-place,
Standing on his own roof or in his garden on a mount
Of twenty-five cubits in height, such space is his Universe;
And on its verge to Sun rises & sets, the Clouds bow
To meet the flat Earth & the Sea I such an order'd Space.
The Starry heavens reach no further, but here bend and set
On all sides, & the two Poles turn on their valves of gold;

And if he move his dwelling-place, his heavens also move
Where'er he goes, & all his neighbourhood bewail his loss.
Such are the Spaces called Earth, & such its dimension.
As to that false appearance which appears to the reasoner,
As of a Globe rolling thro' Voidness, it is a delusion of Ulro.
The Microscope knows not of this, nor the Telescope; they alter
The ratio of the Spectator's Organs, but leave Objects untouch'd.
For every Space larger than a red globule of Man's blood
Is visionary, and is created by the Hammer of Los;
And every Space smaller than a Globule of Man's blood opens
Into Eternity, of which this vegetable Earth is but a shadow.
The red Globule is the unwearied Sun by Los created
To measure Time and Space to mortal Men every morning.
Bowlahoola & Allamanda are placed on each side
Of that Pulsation & that Globule, terrible their power.

* * *

Book the Second

...

PLATE 31

Thou hearest the Nightingale begin the Song of Spring.
The Lark sitting upon his earthly bed, just as the morn
Appears, listens silent, then springing from the waving Corn-field! loud
He leads the Choir of Day! trill, trill, trill, trill,
Mounting upon the wings of light into the great Expanse,
Reecchoing against the lovely blue & shining heavenly Shell.
His little throat labours with inspiration; every feather
On throat & breast & wings vibrates with the effluence Divine.
All Nature listens silent to him, & the awful Sun
Stands still upon the Mountain looking on this little Bird
With eyes of soft humility & wonder, love & awe.
Then loud from their green covert all the Birds begin their Song:
The Thrush, the Linnet & the Goldfinch, Robin & the Wren
Awake the Sun from his sweet reverie upon the Mountain,

The Nightingale again assays his song, & thro' the day
And thro' the night warbles luxuriant: every Bird of Song
Attending his loud harmony with admiration & love.
This is a Vision of the lamentation of Beulah over Ololon.
Thou perceivest the Flowers put forth their precious Odours,
And none can tell how from so small a center comes such sweet,
Forgetting that within that Center Eternity expands
Its ever during doors that Og & Anak fiercely guard.
First e'er the morning breaks joy opens in the flowery bosoms,
Joy even to tears, which the Sun rising dries; first the Wild Thyme
And Meadow-sweet, downy & soft, waving among the reeds,
Light springing on the air, lead the sweet Dance: they wake
The Honeysuckle sleeping on the Oak; the flaunting beauty
Revels along upon the wind; the White-thorn, lovely May,
Opens her many lovely eyes; listening the Rose still sleeps—
None dare to wake her, soon she bursts her crimson curtain'd bed
And comes forth in the majesty of beauty; every Flower,
The Pink, the Jessamine, the Wall-flower, the Carnation
The Jonquil, the mild Lilly opes her heavens; every Tree
And Flower & Herb soon fill the air with an innumerable Dance,
Yet all in order sweet & lovely. Men are sick with Love.
Such is a Vision of the lamentation of Beulah over Ololon.

PLATE 32

And Milton oft sat up on the Couch of Death, & oft conversed
In vision & dream beatific with the Seven Angels of the Presence:
I have turned my back upon these Heavens builded on cruelty.
My Spectre still wandering thro' them follows my Emanation;
He hunts her footsteps thro' the snow & the wintry hail & rain.
The idiot Reasoner laughs at the Man of Imagination,
And from laughter proceeds to murder by undervaluing calumny'.
Then Hillel, who is Lucifer, replied over the Couch of Death,
And thus the Seven Angels instructed him & thus they converse:

'We are not Individuals but States, Combinations of Individuals.
We were Angels of the Divine Presence, & were Druids in Annandale,
Compell'd to combine into Form by Satan, the Spectre of Albion,
Who made himself a God & destroyed the Human Form Divine.
But the Divine Humanity & Mercy gave us a Human Form
Because we were combin'd in Freedom & holy Brotherhood;
While those combin'd by Satan's Tyranny, first in the blood of War
And Sacrifice & next in Chains of imprisonment, are Shapeless Rocks
Retaining only Satan's Mathematic Holiness, Length, Bredth & Highth,
Calling the Human Imagination, which is the Divine Vision & Fruition
In which Man liveth eternally, madness & blasphemy, against
Its own Qualities, which are Servants of Humanity, not Gods or Lords.
Distinguish therefore States from Individuals in those States.
States change, but Individual Identities never change nor cease.
You cannot go to Eternal Death in that which can never Die.
Satan & Adam are States Created into Twenty-seven Churches,
And thou, O Milton, art a State about to be Created
Called Eternal Annihilation, that none but the Living shall
Dare to enter; & they shall enter triumphant over Death
And Hell & the Grave: States that are not, but ah! Seem to be.
'Judge then of thy Own Self: thy Eternal Lineaments explore,
What is Eternal & what Changeable, & what Annihilable?
The Imagination is not a State: it is the Human Existence itself.
Affection or Love becomes a State when divided from Imagination.
The Memory is a State always, & the Reason is a State
Created to be Annihilated & a new Ratio Created.
Whatever can be Created can be Annihilated: Forms cannot.
The Oak is cut down by the Ax, the Lamb falls by the Knife.
But their Forms Eternal Exist For-ever. Amen. Hallelujah?

Thus they converse with the Dead, watching round the Couch of Death.
For God himself enters Death's Door always with those that enter,
And lays down in the Grave with them, in Visions of Eternity,
Till they awake & see Jesus, & the Linen Clothes lying
That the Females had Woven for them, & the Gates of their Father's House.

* * *

PLATE 35

There is a Moment in each Day that Satan cannot find,
Nor can his Watch Fiends find it; but the Industrious find
This Moment & it multiply; & when it once is found
It renovates every Moment of the Day if rightly placed.
In this Moment Ololon descended to Los & Enitharmon,
Unseen beyond the Mundane Shell, Southward in Milton's track.
Just in this Moment when the morning odours rise abroad,
And first from the Wild Thyme, stands a Fountain in a rock
Of crystal flowing into two Streams: one flows thro' Golgonooza
And thro' Beulah to Eden beneath Los's western Wall;
The other flows thro' the Aerial Void & all the Churches,
Meeting again in Golgonooza beyond Satan's Seat.

The Wild Thyme is Los's Messenger to Eden, a mighty Demon,
Terrible, deadly & poisonous his presence in Ulro dark;
Therefore he appears only a small Root creeping in grass,
Covering over the Rock of Odours his bright purple mantle
Beside the Fount above the Lark's Nest in Golgonooza.
Luvah slept here in death, & here is Luvah's empty Tomb.
Ololon sat beside this Fountain on the Rock of Odours.

Just at the place to where the Lark mounts is a Crystal Gate:
It is the enterance of the First Heaven, named Luther for
The Lark is Los's Messenger thro' the Twenty-seven Churches,
That the Seven Eyes of God, who walk even to Satan's Seat
Thro' all the Twenty-seven Heavens, may not slumber nor sleep.

But the Lark's Nest is at the Gate of Los, at the eastern
Gate of wide Golgonooza, & the Lark is Los's Messenger.

PLATE 36

When on the highest lift of his light pinions he arrives
At that bright Gate, another Lark meets him, & back to back
They touch their pinions, tip tip, and each descend
To their respective Earths, & there all night consult with Angels
Of Providence & with the eyes of God all night in slumbers
Inspired & at the dawn of day send out another Lark
Into another Heaven to carry news upon his wings.
Thus are the Messengers dispatch'd till they reach the Earth again
In the East Gate of Golgonooza; & the Twenty-eighth bright
Lark met the Female Ololon descending into my Garden.
Thus it appears to Mortal eyes & those of the Ulro Heavens,
But not thus to Immortals; the Lark is a mighty Angel.
For Ololon step'd into the Polypus within the Mundane Shell—
They could not step into Vegetable Worlds without becoming
The enemies of Humanity, except in a Female Form—
And as One Female Ololon and all its mighty Hosts
Appear'd: a Virgin of twelve years. Nor time nor space was
To the perception of the Virgin Ololon; but as the
Flash of lightning, but more quick, the Virgin in my Garden
Before my Cottage stood for the Satanic Space is delusion.
For when Los join'd with me he took me in his fiery whirlwind.
My Vegetated portion was hurried from Lambeth's shades
He set me down in Felpham's Vale & prepar'd a beautiful
Cottage for me, that in three years I might write all these Visions
To display Nature's cruel holiness, the deceits of Natural Religion.
Walking in my Cottage Garden sudden I beheld
The Virgin Ololon & address'd her as a Daughter of Beulah.

Virgin of Providence, fear not to enter into my Cottage
What is thy message to thy friend? What am I now to do?
Is it again to plunge into deeper affliction? Behold me
Ready to obey, but pity thou my Shadow of Delight
Enter my Cottage, comfort her, for she is sick with fatigue.'

PLATE 37

The Virgin answer'd: Knowest thou of Milton who descended
Driven from Eternity. Him I seek terrified at my Act
In Great Eternity which thou knowest, I come him to seek'.
So Ololon utter'd in words distinct the anxious thought:
Mild was the voice, but more distinct than any earthly.
That Milton's Shadow heard; & condensing all his Fibres
Into a strength impregnable of majesty & beauty infinite,
I saw he was the Covering Cherub & within him Satan
And Rahab, in an outside which is fallacious, within
Beyond the outline of Identity in the Selfhood deadly.
And he appear'd the Wicker Man of Scandinavia, in whom
Jerusalem's children consume in flames among the Stars.

Descending down into my Garden' a Human Wonder of God
Reaching from heaven to earth, a Cloud & Human Form,
I beheld Milton with astonishment, & in him beheld
The Monstrous Churches of Beulah, the Gods of Ulro dark
Twelve monstrous dishumaniz'd terrors. Synagogues of Satan,
A Double Twelve & Thrice Nine: such their divisions.

* * *

PLATE 38

And Milton, colleding all his fibres into impregnable strength,
Descended down a Paved work of all kinds of precious stones
Out from the eastern sky; descending down into my Cottage
Garden, clothed in black, severe & silent he descended.

The Spectre of Satan stood upon the roaring sea & beheld
Milton within his sleeping Humanity; trembling & shudd'ring
He stood upon the waves, a Twenty-seven-fold mighty Demon,
Gorgeous & beautiful; loud roll his thunders against Milton.
Loud Satan thunder'd, loud & dark upon mild Felpham shore;
Not daring to touch one fibre he howl'd round upon the Sea.
I also stood in Satan's bosom & beheld its desolations:
A ruin'd Man, a ruin'd building of God, not made with hands;
Its plains of burning sand, its mountains of marble terrible;
Its pits & declivities flowing with molten ore & fountains
Of pitch & nitre; its ruin'd palaces & cities & mighty works;

Its furnaces of affliction, in which his Angels & Emanations
Labour with blacken'd visages among its stupendous ruins,
Arches & pyramids & porches, colonades & domes,
In which dwells Mystery, Babylon, here is her secret place;
From hence she comes forth in the Churches in delight;
Here is her cup fill'd with its poisons, in these horrid vales,
And here her scarlet Veil woven, in pestilence & war;
Here is Jerusalem bound in chains in the Dens of Babylon.
In the Eastern porch of Satan's Universe Milton stood & said:
'Satan! my Spectre! I know my power thee to annihilate
And be a greater in thy place, & be thy Tabernacle,
A covering for thee to do thy will, till one greater comes
And smites me as I smote thee & becomes my covering.
Such are the laws of thy false Heav'ns; but Laws of Eternity
Are not such, know thou, I come to Self Annihilation.
Such are the Laws of Eternity, that each shall mutually
Annihilate himself for other's good, as I for thee.
Thy purpose & the purpose of thy Priests & of thy Churches
Is to impress on men the fear of death, to teach
Trembling & fear, terror, constriction, abject selfishness.
Mine is to teach Men to despise death & to go on
In fearless majesty annihilating Self, laughing to scorn
Thy Laws & terrors, shaking down thy Synagogues as webs.
I come to discover before Heav'n & Hell the Self righteousness
In all its Hypocritic turpitude, opening to every eye
These wonders of Satan's holiness, shewing to the Earth
The Idol Virtues of the Natural Heart, & Satan's Seat
Explore in all its Selfish Natural Virtue, & put off
In Self annihilation all that is not of God alone,
To put off Self & all I have, ever & ever. Amen'.

Satan heard, Coming in a cloud with trumpets & flaming fire,
Saying: 'I am God the judge of all, the living & the dead.
Fall therefore down & worship me, submit thy supreme
Dictate to my eternal Will, & to my dictate bow.
I hold the Balances of Right & Just & mine the Sword.
Seven Angels bear my Name & in those Seven I appear;
But I alone am God, & I alone in Heav'n & Earth
Of all that live dare utter this; others tremble & bow;

PLATE 39

Till All Things become One Great Satan, in Holiness
Oppos'd to Mercy, and the Divine Delusion, Jesus, be no more.'

Suddenly around Milton on my Path the Starry Seven
Burn'd terrible! My Path became a solid fire, as bright
As the clear Sun, & Milton silent came down on my Path.
And there went forth from the Starry limbs of the Seven, Forms
Human, with Trumpets innumerable, sounding articulate
As the Seven spake; and they stood in a mighty Column of Fire
Surrounding Felpham's Vale, reaching to the Mundane Shell, Saying:

'Awake, Albion awake ! reclaim thy Reasoning Spectre. Subdue
Him to the Divine Mercy; Cast him down into the Lake
Of Los that ever burneth with fire, ever & ever, Amen!
Let the Four Zoas awake from Slumbers of Six Thousand Years'.
Then loud the Furnaces of Los were heard; & seen as Seven Heavens
Stretching from south to north over the mountains of Albion.
Satan heard; trembling round his Body, he incircled it;
He trembled with exceeding great trembling & astonishment,
Howling in his Spectre round his Body, hung'ring to devour
But fearing for the pain, for if he touches a Vital
His torment is unendurable. Therefore he cannot devour,
But howls round it as a lion round his prey continually.
Loud Satan thunder'd, loud & dark upon mild Felpham's Shore,
Coming in a Cloud with Trumpets & with Fiery Flame,
An awful Form eastward, from midst of a bright Paved-work
Of precious stones by Cherubim surrounded, so permitted
(Lest he should fall apart in his Eternal, Death) to imitate
The Eternal Great Humanity Divine surrounded by
His Cherubim & Seraphim in ever happy Eternity.
Beneath sat Chaos: Sin on his right hand Death on his left;
And Ancient Night spread over all the heav'n his Mantle of Laws.
He trembled with exceeding great trembling & astonishment.

Then Albion rose up in the Night of Beulah on his Couch
Of dread repose seen by the visionary eye: his face is toward
The east, toward Jerusalem's Gates; groaning he sat above
His rocks. London & Bath & Legions & Edinburgh
Are the four pillars of his Throne; his left foot near London
Covers the shades of Tyburn; his instep from Windsor;
To Primrose Hill stretching to Highgate & Holloway;
London is between his knees, its basements fourfold:
His right foot stretches to the sea on Dover cliffs, his heel
On Canterbury's ruins; his right hand covers lofty Wales,
His left Scotland; his bosom girt with gold involves
York, Edinburgh, Durham & Carlisle, & on the front
Bath, Oxford, Cambridge, Norwich; his right elbow
Leans on the Rocks of Erin's Land, Ireland, ancient nation;
His head bends over London. He sees his embodied Spectre
Trembling before him with exceeding great trembling & fear.
He views Jerusalem & Babylon, his tears flow down.
He mov'd his right foot to Cornwall, his left to the rocks of Bognor;
He strove to rise to walk into the Deep, but strength failing
Forbad; & down with dreadful groans he sunk upon his Couch
In moony Beulah. Los, his strong Guard, walks round beneath the Moon.
Urizen faints in terror, striving among the Brooks of Arnon
With Milton's Spirit. As the Plowman or Artificer or Shepherd
While in the labours of his Calling sends his Thought abroad
To labour in the ocean or in the starry heaven, So Milton
Labour 'd in Chasms of the Mundane Shell, tho' here before
My Cottage midst the Starry Seven, where the Virgin Ololon
Stood trembling in the Porch. Loud Satan thunder'd on the stormy Sea,
Circling Albion's cliffs in which the Four-fold World resides,
Tho' seen in fallacy outside, a fallacy of Satan's Churches.

PLATE 40

Before Ololon Milton stood & perceiv'd the Eternal Form
Of that mild Vision; wondrous were their acts, by me unknown
Except remotely; and I heard Ololon say to Milton:
I see thee strive upon the Brooks of Arnon. There a dread

And awful Man I see, o'ercover'd with the mantle of years.
I behold Los & Urizen, I behold Orc & Tharmas,
The Four Zoas of Albion, & thy Spirit with them striving,
In Self annihilation giving thy life to thy enemies.
Are those who contemn Religion & seek to annihilate it
Become in their Feminine portions the causes & promoters
Of these Religions. How is this thing, this Newtonian Phantasm,
This Voltaire & Rousseau, this Hume & Gibbon & Bolingbroke,
This Natural Religion, this impossible absurdity?
Is Ololon the cause of this? O where shall I hide my face?
These tears fall for the little ones, the Children of Jerusalem,
Lest they be annihilated in thy annihilation.'

No sooner she had spoke but Rahab Babylon appear'd
Eastward upon the Paved work across Europe & Asia,
Glorious as the midday Sun, in Satan's bosom glowing,
A Female hidden in a Male, Religion hidden in War,
Nam'd Moral Virtue, cruel two-fold Monster shining bright,
A Dragon red & hidden Harlot which John in Patmos saw.

And all beneath the Nations innumerable of Ulro
Apear'd: the Seven Kingdoms of Canaan & Five Baalim
Of Philistea into Twelve divided, call'd after the Names
Of Israel, as they are in Eden—Mountain, River & Plain,
City & sandy Desart intermingled beyond mortal ken.
But turning toward Ololon in terrible majesty, Milton
Replied: 'Obey thou the Words of the Inspired Man.
All that can be annihilated must be annihilated
That the Children of Jerusalem may be saved from slavery.
There is a Negation, & there is a Contrary,
The Negation must be destroy'd to redeem the Contraries.
The Negation is the Spectre the Reasoning Power in Man.
This is a false Body, an Incrustation over my Immortal
Spirit, a Selfhood which must be put off & annihilated alway.
To cleanse the Face of my Spirit by Self-examination,

PLATE 41

To bathe in the Waters of Life, to wash off the Not Human,
I come in Self-annihilation & the grandeur of Inspiration;
To cast off Rational Demonstration by Faith in the Saviour,

To cast off the rotten rags of Memory by Inspiration,
To cast off Bacon, Locke & Newton from Albion's covering.
To take off his filthy garments, & clothe him with Imagination;
To cast aside from Poetry all that is not Inspiration,
That it no longer shall dare to mock with the aspersion of Madness
Cast on the Inspired by the tame high finisher of paltry Blots
Indefinite, or paltry Rhymes, or paltry Harmonies
Who creeps into State Government like a catterpiller to destroy;
To cast off the idiot Questioner who is always questioning,
But never capable of answering, who sits with a sly grin
Silent plotting when to question like a thief in a cave:
Who publishes doubt & calls it knowledge, whose Science is Despair,
Whose pretence to knowledge is Envy, whose whole Science is
To destroy the wisdom of ages to gratify ravenous Envy,
That rages round him like a Wolf day & night without rest.
He smiles with condescension, he talks of Benevolence & Virtue,
And those who act with Benevolence & Virtue they murder time on time.
These are the destroyers of Jerusalem, those are the murderers
Of Jesus, who deny the Faith & mock at Eternal Life;
Who pretend to Poetry that they may destroy Imagination,
By imitation of Nature's Images drawn from Remembrance.
These are the Sexual Garments, the Abomination of Desolation,
Hiding the Human Lineaments as with an Ark & Curtains.
Which Jesus rent & now shall wholly purge away with Fire.
Till Generation is swallow'd up in Regeneration.
Then trembled the Virgin Ololon & reply 'd in clouds of despair:
'Is this our Feminine Portion, the Six-fold Miltonic Female?
Terribly this Portion trembles before thee, O awful Man!
Altho' our Human Power can sustain the severe contentions
Of Friendship, our Sexual cannot, but flies into the Ulro.
Hence arose all our terrors in Eternity; & now remembrance
Returns upon us. Are we Contraries, O Milton, Thou & I?
O Immortal? how were we led to War the Wars of Death?
Is this the Void Outside of Existence, which if enter'd into

PLATE 42

Becomes a Womb? & is this the Death Couch of Albion?
Thou goest to Eternal Death, & all must go with thee'.

So saying, the Virgin divided Six-fold, & with a shriek
Dolorous that ran thro' all Creation, a Double-Six-fold Wonder,
Away from Ololon she divided & fled into the depths
Of Milton's Shadow as a Dove upon the stormy Sea.
Then as a Moony Ark Ololon descended to Felpham's Vale
In clouds of blood, in streams of gore, with dreadful thunderings.
Into the Fires of Intellect that rejoic'd in Felpham's Vale
Around the Starry Eight. With one accord the Starry Eight became
One Man, Jesus the Saviour, wonderful! round his limbs
The Clouds of Ololon folded as a Garment dipped in blood,
Written within & without in woven letters; & the Writing
Is the Divine Revelation in the Litteral expression,
A Garment of War. I heard it nam'd the Woof of Six Thousand Years.

And I beheld the Twenty-four Cities of Albion
Arise upon their Thrones to Judge the Nations of the Earth;
And the Immortal Four in whom the Twenty-four appear Four-fold
Arose around Albion's body. Jesus wept & walked forth
From Felpham's Vale clothed in Clouds of blood, to enter into
Albion's Bosom, the bosom of death, & the Four surrounded him
In the Column of Fire in Felpham's Vale. Then to their mouths the Four
Applied their Four Trumpets & then sounded to the Four winds.

Terror struck in the Vale. I stood at that immortal sound;
My bones trembled. I fell outstretch'd upon the path
A moment, & my Soul return'd into its mortal state,
To Resurrection & Judgment in the Vegetable Body;
And my sweet Shadow of Delight stood trembling by my side.

Immediately the Lark mounted with a loud trill from Felpham's Vale,

And the Wild Thyme from Wimbleton's green & impurpled Hills;
And Los & Enitharmon rose over the Hills of Surrey.
Their clouds roll over London with a south wind. Soft Oothoon
Pants in the Vales of Lambeth, weeping o'er her Human Harvest.
Los listens to the Cry of the Poor Man, his Cloud
Over London in volume terrific, low bended in anger.
Rintrah & Palamabron view the Human Harvest beneath.
Their Wine-presses & Barns stand open; the Ovens are prepar'd:
The Waggons ready; terrific Lions & Tygers sport & play.
All Animals upon the Earth are prepar'd in all their strength

PLATE 43

To go forth to the Great Harvest & Vintage of the Nations.

A VISION OF THE LAST JUDGMENT

This world of imagination is the world of Eternity; it is the divine bosom into which we shall all go after the death of the vegetated body. This World of Imagination is Infinite & Eternal, whereas the world of Generation or vegetation is Finite & temporal. There exist in that Eternal World the Permanent Realities of Every Thing which we see are reflected in this Vegetable Glass of Nature.

All Things are comprehended in their Eternal Forms in the Divine body of the Saviour, the Frue Vine of Eternity, the human imagination, who appear'd to me as Coming to Judgement among his Saints and throwing off the Temporal that the Eternal might be Establish'd.

* * *

Men are admitted into Heaven not because they have curbed & govern'd their Passions or have No but because they have Cultivated their understandings. The Treasures of Heaven are not Negations of Passion, but Realities of Intellect from which all the passions emanate uncurbed in their Eternal Glory. The Fool shall not enter into heaven, let him be ever so Holy. Holiness is not The Price of Enterance into Heaven. Those who are cast out are All

Those who, Having no passions of their own because no intellect, have spent their lives in curbing & governing other people's by the various arts of poverty and cruelty of all kinds. Wo, Wo, Wo to you, hypocrites! Even murder the courts of justice, more merciful than the Church, are compell'd to allow is not done in Passion, but in Cool Blooded design & Intention.

The Modern Church Crucifies Christ with the head Downwards.

* * *

The Last Judgement is an overwhelming of Bad Art & Science. Mental Things are alone Real; what is call'd Corporeal Nobody Knows of its Dwelling Place is a Fallacy & its Existence an Imposture. Where is the Existence Out of Mind or Thought? Where is it but in the Mind of a Fool? Some People flatter themselves that there will be No Last Judgement, & that Bad Art will be adopted and mixed with Good Art, that Error or Experiment will make a part of Truth & they Boast that it is its Foundation, These people flatter themselves. I will not Flatter them. Error is Created; Truth is Eternal. Error or Creation will be Burned up, & then, & not till Then Truth or Eternity will appear. It is Burnt up the Moment Men cease to behold it. I assert for My self that I do not behold the Outward Creation, & that to me it is hindrance & not Action; it is as the Dirt upon my feet, No part of Me. "What," it will be Question'd, "When the sun rises do you not see a round Disk of fire somewhat like a Guinea?' " O' no, no, I see an innumerable company of the heavenly host rying: "Holy, Holy, Holy is the Lord God Almighty." I question not my Corporeal or Vegetative Eye any more than I would Question a Window concerning a Sight. I look through it, & not with it.

JERUSALEM

PLATE 4

Of the Sleep of Ulro! and of the passage through
Eternal Death! and of the awaking to Eternal Life.

This theme calls me in sleep night after night, & ev'ry morn
Awakes me at sun-rise then I see the Saviour over me
Spreading his beams of love & dictating the words of this mild song:
'Awake! awake, O sleeper of the land of shadows, wake! expand!
I am in you and you in me, mutual in love divine:
Fibres of love from man to man thro' Albion's pleasant land.
In all the dark Atlantic vale, down from the hills of Surrey,
A black water accumulates. Return, Albion, return!
Thy brethren call thee and thy fathers and thy sons,
Thy nurses and thy mothers, thy sisters and thy daughters
Weep at thy soul's disease, and the Divine Vision is darken'd.
Thy Emanation that was wont to play before thy face,
Beaming forth with her daughters into the Divine bosom
Where hast thou hidden thy Emanation, lovely Jerusalem,
From the vision and fruition of the Holy-one?
I am not a God afar off, I am a brother and friend;
Within your bosoms I reside, and you reside in me.
Lo! we are One, forgiving all Evil, Not seeking recompense.
Ye are my members, O ye sleepers of Beulah, land of shades!'
But the perturbed Man away turns down the valleys dark:
'Phantom of the over heated brain! shadow of immortality!
Seeking to keep my soul a victim to thy Love! which binds
Man, the enemy of man, into deceitful friendships
Jerusalem is not; her daughters are indefinite.
By demonstration man alone can live, and not by faith.
My mountains are my own, and I will keep them to myself:
The Malvern and the Cheviot, the Wolds, Plinlimmon & Snowdon
Are mine. here will I build my Laws of Moral Virtue.
Humanity shall be no more, but war & princedom & victory'
So spoke Albion in jealous fears, hiding his Emanation

Upon the Thames and Medway, rivers of Beulah: dissembling
His jealousy before the throne divine, darkening, cold!

* * *

PLATE 5

Trembling I sit day and night; my friends are astonish'd at me,
Yet they forgive my wanderings. I rest not from my great task!
To open the Eternal Worlds, to open the immortal Eyes
Of Man inwards into the Worlds of Thought, into Eternity
Ever expanding in the Bosom of God, the Human Imagination
O Saviour pour upon me thy Spirit of meekness & love;
Annihilate the Selfhood in me, be thou all my life!
Guide thou my hand, which trembles exceedingly upon the rock of ages,
While I write of the building of Golgonooza, & of the terrors of Entuthon;
Of Hand & Hyle & Coban, of Kwantok, Peachey, Brereton, Slayd & Hutton;
Of the terrible sons & daughters of albion and their Generations.

* * *

PLATE 15

I see the Four-fold Man, The Humanity in deadly sleep
And its fallen Emanation, The Spectre & its cruel Shadow.
I see the Past, Present & Future existing all at once
Before me. O Divine Spirit, sustain me on thy wings!
That I may awake Albion from his long & cold repose!
For Bacon & Newton, sheath'd in dismal steel, their terrors hang
Like iron scourges over Albion. Reasonings like vast Serpents
Infold around my limbs, bruising my minute articulations.

I turn my eyes to the Schools & Universities of Europe
And there behold the Loom of Locke, whose Woof rages dire
Wash'd by the Water-wheels of Newton. Black the cloth
In heavy wreathes folds over every Nation. Cruel Works
Of many Wheels I view, wheel without wheel, with cogs tyrannic

Moving by compulsion each other, not as those in Eden, which
Wheel within Wheel in freedom revolve in harmony & peace.

* * *

PLATE 27

The fields from Islington to Marybone,
To Primrose Hill and Saint John's Wood,
Were builded over with pillars of gold,
And there Jerusalem's pillars stood.

Her Little-ones ran on the fields,
The Lamb of God among them seen,
And fair Jerusalem his Bride,
Among the little meadows green.

Pancrass & Kentish-town repose
Among her golden pillars high,
Among her golden arches which
Shine upon the starry sky.
The Jew's-harp-house & the Green Man,
The Pond's where Boys to bathe delight,
The fields of Cows by Willan's farm,
Shine in Jerusalems pleasant sight.

She walks upon our meadows green,
The Lamb of God walks by her side,
And every English Child is seen
Children of Jesus & his Bride,

Forgiving trespasses and sins
Lest Babylon with cruel Og
With Moral & Self-righteous Law
Should Crucify in Satans Synagogue!

What are those golden Builders doing
Near mournful ever-weeping Paddington,
Standing above that mighty Ruin
Where Satan the first victory won

Where Albion slept beneath the Fatal Tree,
And the Druids' golden Knife
Rioted in human gore,
In Offerings of Human Life?

They groan'd aloud on London Stone,
They groan'd aloud on Tyburn's Brook;
Albion gave his deadly groan,
And all the Atlantic Mountains shook.

Albion's Spectre from his Loins.
Tore forth in all the pomp of War.
Satan his name; in flames of fire
He stretch'd his Druid Pillars far.

Jerusalem fell from Lambeth's Vale
Down thro' Poplar & Old Bow,
Thro' Malden & acros the Sea,
In War & howling, death & woe.

The Rhine was red with human blood,
The Danube roll'd a purple tide,
On the Euphrates Satan stood,
And over Asia stretch'd his pride.
He wither'd up sweet Zion's Hill
From every Nation of the Earth;
He wither'd up Jerusalem's Gates,
And in a dark Land gave her birth.

He wither'd up the Human Form
By laws of sacrifice for sin,
Till it became a Mortal Worm,
But O! translucent all within.

The Divine Vision still was seen,
Still was the Human Form, Divine
Weeping in weak & mortal clay,
O Jesus, still the Form was thine.

And thine the Human Face, & thine
The Human Hands & Feet & Breath,
Entering thro' the Gates of Birth
And passing thro' the Gates of Death.

And O thou Lamb of God, whom I
Slew in my dark self-righteous pride,
Art thou return'd to Albion's Land,
And is Jerusalem thy Bride?

Come to my arms & never more

Depart, but dwell for ever here;
  Create my Spirit to thy Love.
Subdue my Spectre to thy Fear.

  Spectre of Albion! warlike Fiend!
In clouds of blood & ruin roll'd.
  I here reclaim thee as my own,
My Selfhood! Satan! arm'd in gold.

  Is this thy soft Family-Love,
Thy cruel Patriarchal pride,
  Planting thy Family alone,
Destroying all the World beside?

  A man's worst enemies are those
Of his own house & family;
  And he who makes his law a curse,
By his own law shall surely die.
  In my Exchanges every Land
Shall walk, & mine in every Land
  Mutual shall build Jerusalem,
Both heart in heart & hand in hand.

* * *

PLATE 31

Fearing that Albion should turn his back against the Divine Vision,
Los took his globe of fire to search the interiors of Albion's
Bosom, in all the terrors of friendship entering the caves
Of despair & death, to search the tempters out, walking among
Albion's rocks & precipices, caves of solitude & dark despair;
And saw every Minute Particular of Albion degraded & murder'd.
But saw not by whom; they were hidden within in the minute particulars
Of which they had possessd themselves; and there they take up
The articulations of a man's soul and laughing throw it down

Into the frame, then knock it out upon the plank, & souls are bak'd
In bricks to build the pyramids of Heber & Terah. But Los
Search'd in vain; clos'd from the minutia he walk'd, difficult.
He came down from Highgate thro' Hackney & Holloway towards London
Till he came to old Stratford & thence to Stepney & the Isle
Of Leutha's Dogs, thence thro' the narrows of the River's side,
And saw every minute particular, the jewels of Albion, running down
The kennels of the streets & lanes as if they were abhorr'd
Every Universal Form was become barren mountains of Moral
Virtue, and every Minute Particular harden'd into grains of sand,
And all the tendernesses of the soul cast forth as filth & mire,
Among the winding places of deep contemplation intricate
To where the Tower of London frown'd dreadful over Jerusalem.
A building of Luvah, builded in Jerusalem's eastern gate to be
His secluded Court. Thence to Bethlehem where was builded
Dens of despair in the house of bread, enquiring in vain
Of stones and rocks he took his way, for human form was none;
And thus he spoke, looking on Albion's City with many tears:
What shall I do? what could I do, if I could find these Criminals?
I could not dare to take vengeance for all things are so constructed
And builded by the Divine hand that the sinner shall always escape,
And he who takes vengeance; alone is the criminal of Providence.
If I should dare to lay my finger on a grain of sand
In way of vengeance. I punish the already punish'd. O whom
Should I pity if I pity not the sinner who is gone astray?
O Albion, if thou takest vengeance, if thou revengest thy wrongs,
Thou art for ever lost! What can I do to hinder the Sons
Of Albion from taking vengeance? or how shall I them perswade?'

So spoke Los, travelling thro' darkness & horrid solitude.
And he beheld Jerusalem in Westminster & Marybone.
Among the ruins of the Temple, and Vala who is her Shadow,
Jerusalem's Shadow bent northward over the Island white,

* * *

PLATE 38

Turning from Universal Love, petrific as he went,
His cold against the warmth of Eden rag'd with loud
Thunders of deadly war (the fever of the human soul),
Fires and clouds of rolling smoke. But mild the Saviour follow'd him,
Displaying the Eternal vision, the Divine Similitude,
In loves and tears of brothers, sisters, sons, fathers, and friends,
Which if Man ceases to behold, he ceases to exist,
Saying: 'Albion! Our wars are wars of life, & wounds of love.
With intellectual spears & long winged arrows of thought.
Mutual in one another's love and wrath all renewing
We live as One Man; for contracting our infinite senses
We behold multitude; or expanding, we behold as one,
As One Man all the Universal Family; and that One Man
We call Jesus the Christ; and he in us, and we in him
Live in perfect harmony in Eden, the land of life
Giving, receiving, and forgiving each others trespasses.
He is the Good shepherd, he is the Lord and master,
He is the Shepherd of Albion, he is all in all
In Eden, in the garden of God, and in heavenly Jerusalem.
If we have offended, forgive us take not vengeance against us'.

* * *

PLATE 52

I saw a Monk of Charlemaine
Arise before my sight;
I talk'd to the Grey as where we stood
In beams of infernal light.

Gibbon arose with a lash of steel
And Voltaire with a wracking wheel;

The Schools, in clouds of learning roll'd,
Arose with War in iron & gold.

'Thou lazy Monk,' they said afar,
'In vain condemning glorious War!
And in thy Cell thou shall ever dwell:
Rise, War, & bind him in his Cell!'

The blood red ran from the Grey Monk's side;
His hands & feet were wounded wide,
His body bent, his arms & knees
Like to the roots of ancient trees.

When Satan first the black bow bent
And the Moral Law from the Gospel rent,
He forg'd the Law into a Sword
And spill'd the blood of mercy's Lord.
Titus! Constantine! Charlemaine!
O Voltaire! Rousseau! Gibbon! Vain
Your Grecian Mocks and Roman Sword
Against this image of his Lord!

For a Tear is an Intellectual thing,
And a Sigh is the Sword of an Angel King,
And the bitter groan of the Martyr's woe
Is an Arrow from the Almightie's Bow.

* * *

PLATE 60

But the Divine Lamb stood beside Jerusalem; oft she saw
The lineaments Divine & oft the Voice heard, & oft she said:
'O Lord & Saviour, have the Gods of the Heathen pierced thee?
Or hast thou been pierced in the House of thy Friends?
Art thou alive, & livest thou for-evermore? Or art thou
Not—but a delusive shadow, a thought that liveth not?
Babel mocks, saying there is no God nor Son of God
That thou, O Human Imagination, O Divine Body, art all
A delusion, but I know thee, O Lord, when thou arisest upon
My weary eyes, even in this dungeon & this iron mill.
The Stars of Albion cruel rise; thou bindest to sweet influences,
For thou also sufferest with me, altho' I behold thee not;

And altho I sin & blaspheme thy holy name, thou pitiest me,
Because thou knowest I am deluded by the turning mills
And by these visions of pity & love because of Albion's death
Thus spake Jerusalem, & thus the Divine Voice replied:
'Mild Shade of Man, pitiest thou these Visions of terror & woe?
Give forth thy pity & love; fear not! lo, I am with thee always.
Only believe in me that I have power to raise from death
Thy Brother who Sleepeth in Albion; fear not, trembling Shade.

* * *

PLATE 61

Behold in the Visions of Elohim Jehovah, behold Joseph & Mary
And be comforted, O Jerusalem, in the Visions of Jehovah Elohim.'
She looked & saw Joseph the Carpenter in Nazareth, & Mary
His espoused Wife. And Mary said, 'If thou put me away from thee,
Dost thou not murder me?' Joseph spoke in anger & fury, Should I
Marry a Harlot & an Adulteress?, Mary answer'd, 'Art thou more pure
Than thy Maker, who forgiveth Sins & calls again Her that is Lost?
Tho' She hates, he calls her again in love. I love my dear Joseph,
But he driveth me away from his presence, yet I hear the voice of God
In the voice of my Husband; tho' he is angry for a moment, he will not
Utterly cast me away. If I were pure, never could I taste the sweets
Of the Forgiveness of Sins; if I were holy, I never could behold the tears
Of love of him who loves me in the midst of his anger in furnace of fire.'
'Ah my Mary!' said Joseph, weeping over & embracing her closely in
His arms, Doth he forgive Jerusalem, & not exact Purity from her who is

Polluted? I heard his voice in my sleep & his Angel in my dream,
Saying "Doth Jehovah Forgive a Debt only on condition that it shall
Be Payed? Doth he Forgive Pollution only on conditions of Purity ?
That Debt is not Forgiven! That Pollution is not Forgiven!
Such is the Forgiveness of the Gods, the Moral Virtues of the
Heathen, whose tender Mercies are Cruelty. But Jehovah's Salvation
Is without Money & without Price, in the Continual Forgiveness of Sins,
In the Perpetual Mutual Sacrifice in Great Eternity. For behold,
There is none that liveth & Sinneth not! And this is the Covenant
Of Jehovah: If you Forgive one-another, so shall Jehovah Forgive You,
That He Himself may Dwell among You. Fear not then to take
To thee Mary thy Wife, for she is with Child by the Holy Ghost'"
Then Mary burst forth into a Song; she flowed like a River of
Many Streams in the arms of Joseph & gave forth her tears of joy
Like many waters, and Emanating into gardens & palaces upon
Euphrates, & to forests & floods & animals wild & tame from
Gihon to Hiddekel, & to corn fields & villages & inhabitants
Upon Pison & Arnon & Jordan. And I heard the voice among
The Reapers, Saying, 'Am I Jerusalem the lost Adulteress? or am I
Babylon come up to Jerusalem?' And another voice answer'd Saying:
'Does the voice of my Lord call me again? am I pure thro' his Mercy
And Pity? Am I become lovely as a Virgin in his sight, Who am
Indeed a Harlot drunken with the Sacrifice of Idols? Does he
Call her pure as he did in the days of her Infancy, when She
Was cast out to the loathing of her person? The Chaldean took
Me from my Cradle. The Amalekite stole me away upon his Camels

Before I had ever beheld with love the Face of Jehovah, or known

That there was a God of Mercy. O Mercy, O Divine Humanity!

O Forgiveness & Pity & Compassion! If I were Pure I should never

Have known Thee; If I were Unpolluted I should never have

Glorified thy Holiness, or rejoiced in thy great Salvation.'

Mary leaned her side against Jerusalem. Jerusalem received

The Infant into her hands in the Visions of Jehovah. Times passed on.

Jerusalem fainted over the Cross & Sepulcher. She heard the voice:

'Wilt thou make Rome thy Patriarch Druid, & the Kings of Europe his

Horsemen? Man in the Resurrection changes his Sexual Garments at Will.

Every Harlot was once a Virgin, every Criminal an Infant Love.

PLATE 62

Repose on me till the morning of the Grave. I am thy life'.

Jerusalem replied. 'I am an outcast; Albion is dead.
I am left to the trampling foot & the spurning heel;
A Harlot I am call'd; I am sold from street to street'
I am defaced with blows & with the dirt of the Prison.
And wilt thou become my Husband, O my Lord & Saviour?
Shall Vala bring thee forth? shall the Chaste be ashamed also?
I see the Maternal Line, I behold the Seed of the Woman:
Cainah & Ada & Zillah & Naamah, Wife of Noah,
Shuah's daughter & Tamar & Rahab the Canaanites,
Ruth the Moabite & Bathsheba of the daughters of Heth,
Naamah the Ammonite, Zibeah the Philistine, & Mary.
These are the Daughters of Vala, Mother of the Body of death.
But I thy Magdalen behold thy Spiritual Risen Body.
Shall Albion arise? I know he shall arise at the Last Day.
I know that in my flesh I shall see God: but Emanations
Are weak, they know not whence they are, nor whither tend.
Jesus replied, I am the Resurrection & the Life.
I Die & pass the limits of possibility, as it appears
To individual perception. Luvah must be Created

And Vala; for I cannot leave them in the gnawing Grave,
But will prepare a way for my banished-ones to return.
Come now with me into the villages, walk thro' all the cities.
Tho' thou art taken to prison & judgment, starved in the streets,
I will command the cloud to give thee food & the hard rock
To flow with milk & wine, tho' thou seest me not a season,
Even a long season, & a hard journey & a howling wilderness.
Tho' Vala's cloud hide thee & Luvah's fires follow thee,
Only believe & trust in me. Lo, I am always with thee'.

So spoke the Lamb of God, while Luvah's Cloud reddening above
Burst forth in streams of blood upon the heavens, & dark night
Involv'd Jerusalem; & the Wheels of Albion's Sons turn'd hoarse
Over the Mountains, & the fires blaz'd on Druid Altars,
And the Sun set in Tyburn's Brook where Victims howl & cry.
But Los beheld the Divine Vision among the flames of the Furnaces.
Therefore he lived & breathed in hope; but his tears fell incessant
Because his Children were clos'd from him apart, & Enitharmon
Dividing in fierce pain. Also the Vision of God was clos'd in clouds
Of Albion's Spectres, that Los in despair oft sat & often ponder'd,
On Death Eternal, in fierce shudders upon the mountains of Albion
Walking, & in the vales in howlings fierce. Then to his Anvils
Turning, anew began his labours, tho' in terrible pains.

* * *

PLATE 65

Then left the Sons of Urizen the plow & harrow, the loom,
The hammer & the chisel & the rule & compasses; from London fleeing,
They forg'd the sword on Cheviot, the chariot of war & the battle-ax,
The trumpet fitted to mortal battle, & the flute of summer in Annandale.

And all the Arts of Life they chang'd into the Arts of Death in Albion:
The hour-glass contemn'd because its simple workmanship
Was like the workmanship of the plowman, & the water wheel
That raises water into cisterns broken & burn'd with fire
Because its workmanship was like the workmanship of the shepherd.
And in their stead, intricate wheels invented, wheel without wheel,
To perplex youth in their outgoings & to bind to labours in Albion
Of day & night the myriads of eternity; that they may grind
And polish brass & iron hour after hour, laborious task,
Kept ignorant of its use; that they might spend the days of wisdom
In sorrowful drudgery to obtain a scanty pittance of bread;
In ignorance to view a small portion & think that All,
And call it Demonstration, blind to all the simple rules of life.

* * *

PLATE 90

But still the thunder of Los peals loud, & thus the thunders cry:
'These beautiful Witchcrafts of Albion are gratifyd by Cruelty.

PLATE 91

It is easier to forgive an Enemy than to forgive a Friend.
The man who permits you to injure him deserves your vengeance;
He also will receive it. Go Spectre! obey my most secret desire,
Which thou knowest without my speaking. Go to these Fiends of Righteousness.
Tell them to obey their Humanities & not pretend Holiness
When they are murderers, as far as my Hammer & Anvil permit.
Go, tell them that the worship of God is honouring his gifts
In other men, & loving the greatest men best, each according
To his Genius, which is the Holy Ghost in Man. There is no other

God than that God who is the intellectual fountain of Humanity.
He who envies or calumniates, which is murder & cruelty,
Murders the Holy-one. Go, tell them this, & overthrow their cup,
Their bread, their altar-table, their incense & their oath,
Their marriage & their baptism, their burial & consecration.
I have tried to make friends by corporeal gifts but have only
Made enemies: I never made friends but by spiritual gifts,
By severe contentions of friendship & the burning fire of thought.
He who would see the Divinity must see him in his Children:
One first, in friendship & love, then a Divine Family, & in the midst
Jesus will appear; so he who wishes to see a Vision, a perfect Whole,
Must see it in its Minute Particulars, Organized & not as thou,
O Fiend of Righteousness, pretendest; thine is a Disorganized
And snowy cloud, brooder of tempests & destructive War.
You smile with pomp & rigor: you talk of benevolence & virtue;
I act with benevolence & Virtue & get murder'd time after time.
You accumulate Particulars & murder by analyzing, that you
May take the aggregate; & you call the aggregate Moral Law;
And you call that swell'd & bloated Form a Minute Particular.
But General Forms have their vitality in Particulars: & every
Particular is a Man, a Divine Member of the Divine Jesus'.

So Los cried at his Anvil, in the horrible darkness weeping.
The Spectre builded stupendous Works, taking the Starry Heavens
Like to a curtain & folding them according to his will,
Repeating the Smaragdine Table of Hermes to draw Los down
Into the Indefinite, refusing to believe without demonstration.
Los reads the Stars of Albion; the Spectre reads the Voids
Between the Stars, among the arches of Albion's Tomb sublime
Rolling the Sea in rocky paths, forming Leviathan
And Behemoth, the War by Sea enormous & the War
By Land astounding, erecting pillars in the deepest Hell
To reach the heavenly arches. Los beheld undaunted furious
His heav'd Hammer; he swung it round & at one blow,
In unpitying ruin driving down the pyramids of pride,

Smiting the Spectre on his Anvil & the integuments of his Eye
And Ear unbinding in dire pain, with many blows,
Of strict severity self-subduing, & with many tears labouring.
Then he sent forth the Spectre; all his pyramids were grains
Of sand, & his pillars dust on the fly's wing, & his starry
Heavens a moth of gold & silver mocking his anxious grasp.
Thus Los alter'd his Spectre, & every Ratio of his Reason
He alter'd time after time, with dire pain & many tears,
Till he had completely divided him into a separate space.

Terrified Los sat to behold, trembling & weeping & howling:
'I care not whether a Man is Good or Evil; all that I care
Is whether he is a Wise Man or a Fool. Go, put off Holiness
And put on Intellect, or my thund'rous Hammer shall drive thee
To wrath which thou condemnest, till thou obey my voice.'
So Los terrified cries; trembling & weeping & howling: 'Beholding,

PLATE 92

What do I see? The Briton, Saxon, Roman, Norman amalgamating
In my Furnaces into One Nation, the English, & taking refuge
In the Loins of Albion the Canaanite united with the fugitive
Hebrew, whom she divided into Twelve & sold into Egypt,
Then scatter'd the Egyptian & Hebrew to the four Winds.
This sinful Nation Created in our Furnaces & Looms is Albion.

So Los spoke. Enitharmon answer'd in great terror in Lambeth's Vale.

The Poet's Song draws to its period, & Enitharmon is no more.
For if he be that Albion I can never weave him in my Looms;
But when he touches the first fibrous thread, like filmy dew
My Looms will be no more & I, annihilate, vanish for ever.
Then thou wilt Create another Female according to thy Will.

Los answer'd, swift as the shuttle of gold: 'Sexes must vanish & cease
To be when Albion arises from his dread repose, O lovely Enitharmon:
When all their Crimes, their Punishments, their Accusations of Sin,

All their Jealousies, Revenges, Murders, hidings of Cruelty in Deceit
Appear only in the Outward Spheres of Visionary Space and Time,
In the shadows of Possibility, by Mutual Forgiveness for evermore,
And in the Vision & in the Prophecy, that we may Foresee & Avoid
The terrors of Creation & Redemption & Judgment.

* * *

PLATE 94

Albion cold lays on his Rock; storms & snows beat round him,
Beneath the Furnaces & the starry Wheels & the Immortal Tomb;
Howling winds cover him; roaring seas dash furious against him;
In the deep darkness broad lightnings glare, long thunders roll.
The weeds of Death inwrap his hands & feet, blown incessant
And wash'd incessant by the for-ever restless sea-waves foaming abroad
Upon the white Rock. England, a Female Shadow, as deadly damps
Of the Mines of Cornwall & Derbyshire, lays upon his bosom heavy,
Moved by the wind in volumes of thick cloud, returning, folding round
His loins & bosom, unremovable by swelling storms & loud rending
Of enraged thunders. Around them the Starry Wheels of their Giant Sons
Revolve, & over them the Furnaces of Los, & the Immortal Tomb around,
Erin sitting in the Tomb to watch them unceasing night and day.
And the Body of Albion was closed apart from all Nations.
Over them the famish'd Eagle screams on boney Wings, and around

Them howls the Wolf of famine; deep heaves the Ocean black, thundering
Around the wormy Garments of Albion, then pausing in deathlike silence.
Time was Finished! The Breath Divine Breathed over Albion
Beneath the Furnaces & starry Wheels and in the Immortal Tomb,
And England, who is Brittannia, awoke from Death on Albion's bosom:
She awoke pale & cold; she fainted seven times on the Body of Albion:
'O piteous Sleep, O piteous Dream! O God, O God, awake! I have slain
In Dreams of Chastity & Moral Law' I have Murdered Albion! Ah!
In Stone-henge & on London Stone & in the Oak Groves of Malden
I have Slain him in my Sleep with the Knife of the Druid. O England,
O all ye Nations of the Earth behold ye the Jealous Wife!
The Eagle & the Wolf & Monkey & Owl & the King & Priest were there'.

PLATE 95

Her voice pierc'd Albion's clay cold ear he moved upon the Rock.
The Breath Divine went forth upon the morning hills; Albion mov'd
Upon the Rock; he open'd his eyelids in pain, in pain he mov'd
His stony members; he saw England. Ah! shall the Dead live again?
The Breath Divine went forth over the morning hills. Albion rose
In anger, the wrath of God breaking bright flaming on all sides around
His awful limbs. Into the Heavens he walked, clothed in flames,
Loud thund'ring, with broad flashes of flaming lightning & pillars
Of fire, speaking the Words of Eternity in Human Forms, in direful

Revolutions of Action & Passion, thro' the Four Elements on all sides
Surrounding his awful Members. Thou seest the Sun in heavy clouds
Struggling to rise above the Mountains. In his burning hand
He takes his Bow, then chooses out his arrows of flaming gold.
Murmuring the Bowstring breathes with ardor! clouds roll round the
Horns of the wide Bow, loud sounding winds sport on the mountain brows,
Compelling Urizen to his Furrow & Tharmas to his Sheepfold
And Luvah to his Loom. Urthona he beheld mighty labouring at
His Anvil, in the Great Spectre Los unwearied labouring & weeping.
Therefore the Sons of Eden praise Urthona's Spectre in songs,
Because he kept the Divine Vision in time of trouble.
As the Sun & Moon lead forward the Visions of Heaven & Earth,
England, who is Brittannia, enter'd Albion's bosom rejoicing,
Rejoicing in his indignation, adoring his wrathful rebuke.
She who adores not your frowns will only loathe your smiles.

PLATE 96

As the Sun & Moon lead forward the Visions of Heaven & Earth,
England, who is Brittannia, entered Albion's bosom rejoicing.
Then Jesus appeared standing by Albion as the Good Shepherd
By the lost Sheep that he hath found, & Albion knew that it
Was the Lord, the Universal Humanity & Albion saw his Form
A Man, & they conversed as Man with Man; in Ages of Eternity.
And the Divine Appearance was the likeness & similitude of Los:
Albion said. 'O Lord, what can I do? my Selfhood cruel
Marches against thee, deceitful, from Sinai & from Edom
Into the Wilderness of Judah, to meet thee in his pride.
I behold the Visions of my deadly Sleep of Six Thousand Years
Dazling around thy skirts like a Serpent of precious stones & gold

I know it is my Self, O my Divine Creator & Redeemer'.
Jesus replied: 'Fear not, Albion; unless I die thou canst not live,
But if I die I shall arise again & thou with me.
This is Friendship & Brotherhood; without it Man Is Not'.
So Jesus spoke. The Covering Cherub coming on in darkness
Overshadow'd them, & Jesus said: thus do Men in Eternity,
One for another to put off by forgiveness every sin.
Albion reply'd: cannot Man exist without Mysterious
Offering of Self for Another? is this Friendship & Brotherhood?
I see thee in the likeness & similitude of Los my Friend.'
Jesus said: 'Wouldest thou love one who never died
For thee or ever die for one who had not died for thee?
And if God dieth not for Man & giveth not himself
Eternally for Man, Man could not exist; for Man is Love,
As God is Love. Every kindness to another is a little Death
In the Divine Image, nor can Man exist but by Brotherhood.'

So saying, the Cloud overshadowing divided them asunder.
Albion stood in terror, not for himself but for his Friend
Divine, & Self was lost in the contemplation of faith
And wonder at the Divine Mercy & at Los's sublime honour.

'Do I sleep amidst danger to Friends? O my Cities & Counties,
Do you sleep? Rouze up, rouze up! Eternal Death is abroad!
So Albion spoke, & threw himself into the Furnaces of affliction.
All was a Vision, all a Dream! the Furnaces became
Fountains of Living Waters flowing from the Humanity Divine.
And all the Cities of Albion rose from their Slumbers, and All
The Sons & Daughters of Albion on soft clouds, Waking from Sleep.
Soon all around remote the Heavens burnt with flaming fires,
And Urizen & Luvah & Tharmas & Urthona arose into
Albion's Bosom. Then Albion stood before Jesus in the Clouds
Of Heaven, Fourfold among the Visions of God in Eternity:

PLATE 97

'Awake, Awake, Jerusalem! O lovely Emanation of Albion,
Awake and overspread all Nations as in Ancient Time;
For lo! the Night of Death is past and the Eternal Day
Appears upon our Hills! Awake, Jerusalem, and come away!

So spake the Vision of Albion & in him so spake in my hearing
The Universal Father. Then Albion stretch'd his hand into Infinitude,
And took his Bow. Fourfold the Vision: for bright beaming Urizen
Lay'd his hand on the South & took a breathing Bow of carved Gold,
Luvah his hand stretch'd to the East & bore a Silver Bow bright shining;
Tharmas Westward a Bow of Brass pure flaming, richly wrought;
Urthona Northward in thick storms a Bow of Iron, terrible thundering.

And the Bow is a Male & Female, & the Quiver of the Arrows of Love
Are the Children of his Bow, a Bow of Mercy & Loving-kindness, laying
Open the hidden Heart in Wars of mutual Benevolence, Wars of Love;
And the Hand of Man grasps firm between the Male & Female Loves.
And he Clothed himself in Bow & Arrows in awful state, Fourfold
In the midst of his Twenty-eight Cities, each with his Bow breathing.

PLATE 98

Then each an Arrow flaming from his Quiver fitted carefully;
They drew fourfold the unreprovable String, bending thro' the wide Heavens
The horned Bow Fourfold; loud sounding flew the flaming Arrow fourfold.
Murmuring the Bowstring breathes with ardor. Clouds roll round the horns
Of the wide Bow; loud sounding Winds sport on the Mountains' brows.
The Druid Spectre was Annihilate, loud thund'ring, rejoicing terrific, vanishing,
Fourfold Annihilation; & at the clangor of the Arrows of Intellect

The innumerable Chariots of the Almighty appear'd in Heaven,
And Bacon & Newton & Locke, & Milton & Shakspear & Chaucer.
A Sun of blood red wrath surrounding heaven on all sides around,
Glorious, incomprehensible by Mortal Man; & each Chariot was Sexual Threefold.
And every Man stood Fourfold, each Four Faces had: One to the West,
One toward the East, One to the South, One to the North, the Horses Fourfold.
And the dim Chaos brighten'd beneath, above, around ! Eyed as the Peacock,
According to the Human Nerves of Sensation, the Four Rivers of the Water of Life.
South stood the Nerves of the Eye; East in Rivers of bliss, the Nerves of the
Expansive Nostrils; West flow'd the Parent Sense, the Tongue; North stood
The labyrinthine Ear. Circumscribing & Circumcising the excrementitious
Husk & Covering into Vacuum evaporating, revealing the lineaments of Man,
Driving outward the Body of Death in an Eternal Death & Resurrection,
Awaking it to Life among the Flowers of Beulah, rejoicing in Unity
In the Four Senses, in the Outline, the Circumference & Form, for ever
In Forgiveness of Sins which is Self Annihilation; it is the Covenant of Jehovah.

The Four Living Creatures, Chariots of Humanity, Divine, Incomprehensible,
In beautiful Paradises expand. These are the Four Rivers of Paradise,
And the Four Faces of Humanity, fronting the Four Cardinal Points
Of Heaven, going forward, forward irresistible from Eternity to Eternity.
And they conversed together in Visionary forms dramatic, which bright

Redounded from their Tongues in thunderous majesty, in Visions,
In new Expanses, creating exemplars of Memory and of Intellect,
Creating Space, Creating Time, according to the wonders Divine
Of Human Imagination, throughout all the Three Regions immense
Of Childhood, Manhood & Old Age; & the all tremendous unfathomable Non Ens
Of Death was seen in regeneration terrific or complacent, varying
According to the subject of discourse; & every Word & every Character
Was Human, according to the Expansion or Contraction, the Translucence or
Opakeness of Nervous fibres. Such was the variation of Time & Space,
Which vary according as the Organs of Perception vary; & they walked
To & fro in Eternity as One Man, reflecting each in each & clearly seen
And seeing, according to fitness & order. And I heard Jehovah speak
Terrific from his Holy Place, & saw the Words of the Mutual Covenant Divine
On Chariots of gold & jewels, with Living Creatures starry & flaming
With every Colour. Lion, Tyger, Horse, Elephant, Eagle, Dove, Fly, Worm
And the all wondrous Serpent clothed in gems & rich array Humanize
In the Forgiveness of Sins according to the Covenant of Jehovah. They Cry:

'Where is the Covenant of Priam, the Moral Virtues of the Heathen?
Where is the Tree of Good & Evil that rooted beneath the cruel heel
Of Albion's Spectre, the Patriarch Druid? Where are all his Human Sacrifices

For Sin in War & in the Druid Temples of the Accuser of Sin, beneath
The Oak Groves of Albion that cover'd the whole Earth beneath his Spectre?
Where are the Kingdoms of the World & all their glory that grew on Desolation,
The Fruit of Albion's Poverty Tree, when the Triple Headed Gog-Magog Giant
Of Albion Taxed the Nations into Desolation, & then gave the Spectrous Oath?'
Such is the Cry from all the Earth, from the Living Creatures of the Earth
And from the great City of Golgonooza in the Shadowy Generation,
And from the Thirty-two Nations of the Earth among the Living Creatures.

PLATE 99

All Human Forms identified, even Tree, Metal, Earth & Stone' all
Human Forms identified, living, going forth, & returning wearied
Into the Planetary lives of Years, Months, Days & Hours; reposing,
And then Awaking into his Bosom in the Life of Immortality.
And I heard the Name of their Emanations: they are named Jerusalem.

The End of the Song
of Jerusalem

FOR THE SEXES
THE GATES OF PARADISE

The Gates of Paradise

Mutual Forgiveness of each Vice,
Such are the Gates of Paradise.
Against the Accuser's chief desire
Who walkd among the Stones of Fire
Jehovah's Finger Wrote the Law,
Then Wept, then rose in Zeal & Awe
And the Dead Corpse from Sinai's heat
Buried beneath his Mercy Seat
O Christians, Christians, tell me Why
You rear it on your Altars high.

* * *

To the Accuser Who Is the God of This World

Truly, My Satan, thou art but a Dunce,
And dost not know the Garment from the Man.
Every Harlot was a Virgin once,
Nor canst thou ever change Kate into Nan.

Tho' thou art Worship'd by the Names Divine
Of Jesus & Jehovah, thou art still
The Son of Morn in weary Night's decline,
The lost Traveller's Dream under the Hill.

THE EVERLASTING GOSPEL

(j)

There is not one Moral Virtue that Jesus Inculcated but Plato & Cicero did Inculcate before him. What then did Christ Inculcate? Forgiveness of Sins. This alone is the Gospel, & this is the Life & Immortality brought to light by Jesus, Even the Covenant of Jehovah, which is This: If you forgive one another your Trespasses so shall Jehovah forgive you, That he himself may dwell among you; but if you Avenge, you Murder the Divine

Image & he cannot dwell among you because you Murder him; he arises Again & you deny that he is Arisen & are blind to Spirit.

(d)

Was Jesus Humble? or did he
Give any Proofs of Humility?
Boast of high Things with Humble tone,
And give with Charity a Stone?
When but a Child he ran away,
And left his parents in dismay.
When they had wander'd three days long
These were the words upon his tongue:
'No Earthly Parents I confess;
I am doing my Father's business.'
When the rich learned Pharisee
Came to consult him secretly,
Upon his heart with Iron pen
He wrote, 'Ye must be born again.'
He was too proud to take a bribe;
He spoke with authority, not like a Scribe.
He says, with most consummate Art,
'Follow me, I am meek & lowly of heart,'
As that is the only way to escape
The Miser's net & the Glutton's trap.
What can be done with such desperate Fools
Who follow after the Heathen Schools?
I was standing by when Jesus died;
What I call'd Humility they call'd Pride.
He who loves his Enemies betrays his Friends;
This surely is not what Jesus intends,
But the sneaking Pride of Heroic Schools
And the Scribes' & Pharisees' Virtuous Rules.
For he acts with honest, triumphant Pride;
And this is the cause that Jesus died.
He did not die with Christian Ease,
Asking pardon of his Enemies.
If he had, Caiaphas would forgive;
Sneaking submission can always live.

He had only to say that God was the devil,
And the devil was God, like a Christian Civil,
Mild Christian regrets to the devil confess
For affronting him thrice in the Wilderness;
He had soon been bloody Caesar's Elf,
And at last he would have been Caesar himself,
Like Dr Priestly & Bacon & Newton.
Poor Spiritual Knowledge is not worth a button,
For thus the Gospel Sir Isaac confutes:
'God can only be known by his Attributes,
And as to the Indwelling of the Holy Ghost
Or of Christ & his Father, it's all a boast
And Pride & Vanity of the imagination,
That disdains to follow this World's Fashion.'
To teach Doubt & Experiment
Certainly as not what Christ meant.
What was he doing all that time,
From twelve years old to manly prime?
Was he then Idle, or the Less
About his Father's business?
Or was his wisdom held in scorn
Before his wrath began to burn
In Miracles throughout the Land,
That quite unnerv'd Caiaphas' hand?
If he had been Antichrist, Creeping Jesus,
He'd have done any thing to please us;
Gone sneaking into Synagogues,
And not us'd the Elders & Priests like dogs,
But Humble as a Lamb or Ass
Obey'd himself to Caiaphas.
God wants not Man to Humble himself:
This is the trick of the ancient Elf.
This is the Race that Jesus ran:
Humble to God, Haughty to Man,
Cursing the Rulers before the People
Even to the temple's highest Steeple;
And when he Humbled himself to God,
Then descended the Cruel Rod:

'If thou humblest thyself, thou humblest me;
Thou also dwell'st in Eternity.
Thou art a Man, God is no more;
Thy own humanity learn to adore,
For that is my Spirit of Life.
Awake! arise to Spiritual Strife,
And thy Revenge abroad display
In terrors at the Last Judgment day.
God's Mercy & Long Suffering
Is but the Sinner to Judgment to bring.
Thou on the Cross for them shalt pray,
And take Revenge at the Last Day.'
Jesus replied, & thunders hurl'd:
'I never will Pray for the World.
Once I did so when I pray'd in the Garden;
I wish'd to take with me a Bodily Pardon.'
Can that which was of woman born,
In the absence of the Morn,
When the Soul fell into Sleep,
And Archangels round it weep,
Shooting out against the Light
Fibres of a deadly night,
Reasoning upon its own dark Fiction,
In Doubt which is Self Contradiction?
Humility is only doubt,
And does the Sun & Moon blot out,
Rooting over with thorns & stems
The buried Soul & all its gems.
This Life's dim Windows of the Soul
Distorts the Heavens from Pole to Pole,
And leads you to Believe a Lie
When you see with, not thro', the Eye,
That was born in a night to perish in a night,
When the Soul slept in the beams of Light.

(e)

Was Jesus Chaste, or did he
Give any Lessons of Chastity?

The morning blush'd fiery red:
Mary was found in Adulterous bed;
Earth groan'd beneath, & Heaven above
Trembled at discovery of Love.
Jesus was sitting in Moses' Chair,
Thy brought the trembling Woman There:
'Moses commands she be ston'd to death'.
What was the sound of Jesus' breath?
He laid His hand on Moses' Law;
The Ancient Heavens, in Silent Awe,
Writ with Cruses from Pole to Pole,
All away began to roll.
The Earth trembling & Naked lay
In secret bed of Mortal Clay,
On Sinai felt the hand divine
Putting back the bloody shrine;
And she heard the breath of God
As she heard by Eden's flood:
'Good & Evil are no more!
Sinai's trumpets, cease to roar!
Cease, finger of God, to write!
The Heavens are not clean in thy Sight;
Thou art Good, & thou Alone,
Nor may the sinner cast on stone.
To be Good only is to be
A Devil, or else a Pharisee.
Thou Angel of the Presence Divine,
That didst create this Body of Mine,
Wherefore has thou writ these Laws
And Created Hell's dark jaws?
My Presence I will take from thee:
A Cold Leper thou shalt be.
Tho' thou wast so pure & bright
That Heaven was Impure in thy Sight,
Tho' thy Oath turn'd Heaven Pale,
Tho' thy Covenant built Hell's Jail,
Tho' thou didst all to Chaos roll
With the Serpent for its soul,

Still the breath Divine does move,
And the breath Divine is Love.
Mary, Fear Not. Let me see
The Seven Devils that torment thee.
Hide not from my Sight thy Sin,
That forgiveness thou maist win.
Has no Man Condemned thee?'
'No Man, Lord' 'Then what is he
Who shall Accuse thee? Come Ye forth,
Fallen fiends of Heav'nly birth
That have forgot your Ancient love
And driven away my trembling Dove.
You shall bow before her feet,
You shall lick the dust for Meat,
And tho' you cannot Love, but Hate,
Shall be beggars at Love's Gate.
What was thy love? Let me see it;
Was it love, or Dark Deceit?'
'Love too long from Me had fled;
'Twas dark deceit, to Earn my bread;
'Twas Covet, or 'twas Custom, or
Some trifle not worth caring for:
That they may call a shame & Sin
Love's temple that God dwelleth in,
And hide in secret hidden Shrine
The Naked Human form divine,
And render that a Lawless thing
On which the Soul Expands its wing.
But this, O Lord, this was my Sin,
When first I let these devils in
In dark pretence to Chastity,
Blaspheming Love, blaspheming thee.
Thence Rose Secret Adulteries,
And thence did Covet also rise.
My sin thou hast forgiven me;
Canst thou forgive my Blasphemy?
Canst thou return to this dark Hell,
And in my burning bosom dwell?

And canst thou die that I may live?
And canst thou Pity & forgive?'
Then Roll'd the shadowy Man away
From the Limbs of Jesus to make them his prey,
An Ever devouring appetite,
Glittering with festering Venoms bright,
Crying: 'Crucify this case of distress,
Who don't keep the secrets of Holiness!
All Mental Powers by Diseases we bind,
But he heals the Deaf & the Dumb & the Blind.
Whom God has afflicted for Secret Ends
He comforts & Heals & calls them Friends.'
But when Jesus was Crucified,
Then was perfected his glitt'ring pride.
In three Nights he devour'd his prey,
And still he devours the Body of Clay;
For dust & Clay is the Serpent's meat,
Which never was made for Man to Eat.

INDEX OF FIRST LINES